Inspired English

Inspired English

Raising Test Scores
and Writing Effectiveness
Through Poetry and Fiction

Lorraine LaCroix

CORWIN PRESS
A Sage Publications Company
Thousand Oaks, California

#56014599

3-16-05

For information:

Corwin Press
A Sage Publications Company
2455 Teller Road
Thousand Oaks, California 91320
www.corwinpress.com

Sage Publications Ltd.
1 Oliver's Yard
55 City Road
London EC1Y 1SP
United Kingdom

Sage Publications India Pvt. Ltd.
B-42, Panchsheel Enclave
Post Box 4109
New Delhi 110 017 India

Printed in the United States of America

Library of Congress Cataloging-in-Publication Data

LaCroix, Lorraine.
Inspired English : Raising test scores and writing effectiveness through poetry and fiction / Lorraine LaCroix.
    p. cm.
Includes bibliographical references and index.
ISBN 0-7619-3110-4 (cloth) — ISBN 0-7619-3111-2 (pbk.)
   1. English language—Study and teaching (Secondary)—United States. 2. Poetry—Study and teaching (Secondary)—United States. I. Title.
LB1631.L219 2005
428'.0071'2—dc22   2004016460

This book is printed on acid-free paper.

04   05   06   07   08   10   9   8   7   6   5   4   3   2   1

Acquisitions Editor:	Kylee Liegl
Editorial Assistant:	Jaime Cuvier
Production Editor:	Laureen A. Shea
Copy Editor:	Elizabeth S. Budd
Typesetter/Designer:	C&M Digitals (P) Ltd.
Indexer:	Pamela Van Huss
Cover Designer:	Anthony Paular

Contents

Preface

Is poetry important? Does it serve any practical purpose? Absolutely. The study of poetry builds vocabulary. It develops critical thinking skills. It promotes rich discussions, rewards close readings, and elevates the rhetorical effectiveness of student writing. Finally, the study of poetry creates a forum whereby the often neglected oral language skill (the stepchild of the language arts) is included as a natural by-product.

Are stories important? When many cannot find the time in a day to do what one must to survive, is it worth our time to read and discuss stories? Absolutely. Time spent reading rich text forces us to consider the questions collectively termed "the human dilemma." These questions, based in philosophical stances and largely rhetorical in nature, have been asked since the beginning of time. We would all agree that there are no simple answers to these questions, just as many times there are no simple answers to the questions raised in real life. In the end, we each are given options and choices. We compare the stories with experiences in our own lives, make judgments, and come to conclusions. In this way, we learn something new from every story we read, and that new knowledge translates into a greater realization of who we are and where we belong. What could be more important?

What about raising test scores? How do the lessons contained in this book address this very real and valid concern of the classroom teacher? Almost every standardized test used in the secondary language arts classroom contains questions that require higher level critical thinking skills. For example, almost all reading comprehension tests ask students to read short passages and then respond to questions about those selections. In almost every case, there are one or more questions that ask the student to make judgments (e.g., What is the best title for this story?) or inferences (e.g., What word best describes the character's feelings?) about the text. Often, when we review a child's test scores from year to year, we find that he or she is missing the same types of questions, questions that require higher level thinking skills, year after year. To be of service to our students, to offer them opportunities to experience success, we must prepare them, even those who still struggle with basic reading skills, to answer those questions by providing them with lessons that challenge the student to go beyond a literal interpretation of text. The poetry and fiction lessons contained in *Inspired English* do exactly that.

Finally, how do the lessons in this book affect writing effectiveness? Most veteran teachers know, and new teachers will soon learn, that a good reader is a good writer. The lessons in *Inspired English* were not designed specifically to teach the nuts and bolts of essay writing, but to provide students with pieces of literature that are models of writings that convey messages in a powerful, creative, or eloquent writing dynamic. Additionally, the pieces contained in *Inspired English* and other examples of rich literature provide students with new syntactical structures and sophisticated vocabulary. Invariably these skills transfer into their own compositions, and young writers move into another rhetorical dimension, a dimension that can never be reached without exposure to and higher level interaction with rich literature.

Chapter 1 of *Inspired English* details my pedagogical philosophy. Chapter 2 outlines the design, purpose, objectives, and materials needed to build effective units of study. Chapter 3 elaborates on the objectives and offers instruction on how to teach two procedural lessons. Chapter 4 contains twelve fully developed lesson plans ready for classroom use. Chapter 5 offers some suggestions for putting the final touches on a poetry unit.

If you are a new teacher, or one unfamiliar with lesson design, I would strongly recommend that you read Chapters 1 through 3 before teaching the lessons contained in Chapter 4. The beginning chapters lay the foundation for these lessons; they enable the teacher to remain focused on the objectives, and they present a rationale for instruction, often a critical factor when speaking with parents and administrators.

My goal has been to present a practical, commonsense approach to the teaching of fiction and poetry. I have made every attempt to present my ideas clearly and succinctly and to make the lessons as reader friendly as possible. *Inspired English* is a book for both the novice teacher and for the veteran teacher. It is a book designed for the classroom teacher and the home-school teacher. It is a book for all teachers who find that there is never enough time in a day. It is a book written by a teacher, for a teacher.

The ideas and lessons presented in this book are not based on empirical data. Rather, they are based on my experience in the classroom. My curriculum never stopped evolving; each year I set aside some ideas and pulled in others. What we teach from year to year should always, in some way, change because we, as well as our students, change. It is what makes teaching so challenging and fulfilling at the same time.

The lessons presented in Chapter 4 contain all the materials necessary for implementation in the average classroom. I have provided sample text to serve as concrete examples. Teachers should draw on the resources in their classrooms to provide further examples.

I would like to add a final word about teaching poetry. Not all language arts teachers are completely comfortable with the genre. I would encourage you to begin with those lessons with which you feel most comfortable, and then discover others together with your class. It has been my experience that this unit will touch and ignite a genuine talent in some of the most unlikely students. Many of these young adults, as much as we try to avoid it, are often lost in the sea of mediocrity. They are not particularly stellar students nor are they great athletes, but they most certainly are poets—and this unit allows them their moment in the sun.

I would like to acknowledge my boys, Matthew and Nicholas, for their patience and support during the writing of this book, and my editor, Kylee Liegl, for her effort and encouragement during the publication process.

Corwin Press gratefully acknowledges the contributions of the following reviewers:

Mary Dooms
Eighth-Grade Literature Teacher
Lake Zurich Middle Schools
Lake Zurich, IL

Katherine Fedor
Title I Reading Teacher
Birdneck Elementary
Virginia Beach, VA

Sherry Lepine
Assistant Principal
Clint Small Middle School
Austin, TX

Jonathan Potter
High School English Teacher
Camden Hills Regional High School
Rockport, ME

Connie Stewart
Eighth-Grade Language Arts Instructor
Bellwood-Antis Middle School
Bellwood, PA

Lorraine Tough
REA Coach
Pittsburgh City Schools
Pittsburgh, PA

Raegan Virgil
High School Language Arts & Special Ed Teacher
Proctor Hug High School
Reno, NV

About the Author

Lorraine LaCroix, a National Board Certified Teacher, is an Educational Consultant for the Long Beach Unified School District in Southern California. In this capacity, she trains new teachers, coaches veteran educators, and provides professional development geared toward improved instructional practices. During her fifteen-year career with the district, she has worked as a classroom and mentor teacher and has served in a number of leadership roles. She has also been active in writing curriculum for the district's vastly diverse population. LaCroix received the district's Carpe Diem Award in 2000, naming her the outstanding middle school teacher of the year. She holds a bachelor's degree in English literature from California State University, Long Beach, and a master's degree in educational management from the University of LaVerne, also in California. She can be contacted by calling (562) 420-2421, or by e-mail: lacroixteach@yahoo.com.

Dedicated to my first muses—the teachers who so generously
shared their experience and wisdom with me . . .
and
to "my" students—it was the passion I discovered in your eyes,
more than any others, that has encouraged me toward this journey's end.

Opening Letter to Reader

Dear Reader:

Allow me to introduce myself. My name is Lorraine LaCroix, and I taught middle school English in an urban school district for thirteen years. Two years ago, I left the classroom to teach and mentor other teachers. I have thoroughly enjoyed my new position and feel that I am still in the business of touching the lives of children, albeit indirectly.

There are, however, so many things I miss now that I do not have my "own" kids. I miss their quirky humor. I miss their enthusiasm. I miss their uncanny ability to truly start each day anew. I miss their innocence, and I miss their smiles. But most of all, I miss the awe, that light that arose in their eyes whenever they discovered something new—about the world or about themselves.

And so, I decided to write a book about a few things I've learned along the way. *Inspired English* is a book about some ways I have learned to turn on that light, a book about a way, through the "inspired" teaching of fiction and poetry, to empower you to do the same in your classroom, with your students.

It is my sincere hope that, in so doing, I may serve as your guide, as you, too, attempt to awaken the muse in the hearts and minds of your students. It is not an easy journey, but certainly an honorable one; it is in a very real way, a gift to your students and the students of tomorrow, and tomorrow, and tomorrow . . .

I wish you well, my fellow traveler.

Lorraine LaCroix

The Plan 1

A journey of a thousand miles begins . . .

Confucius

How should we plan? Is there a "one size fits all" approach? How many steps are involved? Is the process the same, regardless of content or grade level? The answer to all these questions is the same: Successful teachers have a plan. They may not follow it exactly, but they have a plan. For the teacher in Room 102, it may be a ten-step plan, and for the teacher in Room 216, it may be a five-step plan. But make no mistake, regardless of how effortless it may appear, the successful lesson is the planned lesson.

THE HUNTER MODEL

I have worked with many accomplished teachers who are advocates of Madeline Hunter's ten-step lesson plan. In this format, the ten steps of a lesson are planned and then delivered in the following sequence:

Hunter's Ten-Step Lesson Plan

Terminal Objective

Anticipatory Set

Telling Objective

Purpose

Input

Modeling

Checking for Understanding

Guided Practice

Closure

Independent Practice

In this model, the teacher decides what to teach (Terminal Objective/Telling Objective), how to motivate her students to learn (Anticipatory Set), how to define the ultimate justification for the objective (Purpose), which teaching strategies to enlist (Input, Modeling, Checking for Understanding, and Guided Practice), in what manner to end the lesson (Closure), and finally how the student will work with the new skill/information (Independent Practice). It is an excellent teaching model that provides the novice teacher with a practical, concrete example to follow.

THE GENERALIST MODEL

On the other hand, I have worked with other, equally accomplished, educators who use a five-step lesson plan. I refer to this group as the Generalists. Their model is based on five broad steps.

Generalist's Five-Step Lesson Plan

Decide on Content/Skill to be Taught

Prepare the Materials

Teach the Lesson

Assess the Results

Reteach (if necessary)

The planning template used for the lessons presented in Chapter 4 is based on a version of Hunter's Ten-Step Lesson Plan and the Generalist's Five-Step Lesson Plan. A close comparison of the two plans indicates that they have much in common.

Teacher 1 Hunter Model	Teacher 2 Generalist Model
Terminal objective	Content/skill to be taught
	Prepare the materials
Anticipatory set	
Telling objective	Content/skill to be taught
Input	Teach the lesson
Modeling	Teach the lesson
Checking for understanding	Teach the lesson
Guided practice	Teach the lesson
Closure	
Guided practice	
Independent	Teach the lesson
	Assess the results
	Reteach (if necessary)

THE LACROIX MODEL

The two approaches share eleven components that will be included in our new lesson design template. There are four elements—Anticipatory Set, Prepare the Materials, Reteach, and Closure—that the two approaches do not share. Which of these merit inclusion in our new model?

The Generalist's second step, Prepare the Materials, is not specifically itemized in Hunter's model. Experience has taught me that we cannot assume all teachers will simply know to take this critical step. It is not a natural by-product of the planning process, and if not specifically addressed it can seriously affect the success of the lesson. Even our teacher with the big picture, the Generalist, has taken the time to itemize this step, reinforcing the necessity of preparing materials for the lesson. This step will be included in our new lesson design model.

The Hunter model includes an Anticipatory Set, a way to hook the students, to incite them to learn. Is this step important? Absolutely. Simply put, it has often been said that enthusiasm is contagious. Certainly, we have all been moved or called to action by the words of a keynote or motivational speaker, been caught up in the excitement of a playoff basketball game (even if we had little interest in the team during their regular season), or quite simply experienced a better day because of a smile offered by a stranger. In each of these cases, another person, an entity outside of ourselves, often an individual we hardly know, has been able to move us to action—to change an attitude, an allegiance, or even a lifestyle. Enthusiasm, it has been said, can move mountains. If a speaker, a fan, or a stranger we pass on the streets can bring about a change of attitude, certainly it is possible for the teacher to assume the same role in their classroom. Teachers, through their own excitement for learning, can ignite the same passion in their students. This "hook" into learning new content is achieved by tapping into the student's prior knowledge, relating the content to the student's interests, or presenting the content as information that will be useful to the student. The planning of an anticipatory set becomes critical to the success of the lesson and will be included in our new model.

Closure, a planned strategy for ending a lesson, is included in the Hunter model but not the Generalist model. Research has shown that a review of new concepts before moving on to further lessons can be tremendously beneficial when transferring concepts from short- to long-term memory. This step will also be inserted into the new model.

The concept of reteaching is included in the Generalist's model, but not in Hunter's model. Hunter teachers do not include this piece because they may consider this step an outlier, one that is apart from the lesson they are currently planning. In this instance, and as previously stated, the reteach is included in the formulation of the terminal objective for the following lesson. Advocates of the Generalist's model, however, would contend that this step is so critical to the process of learning that it must be included and specifically addressed in each lesson plan. They would argue also that, faced with the breadth and complexity of the content teachers are urged to "get through" in an academic year, they may well feel the pressure to move on and cover ground rather than return to, and reteach, what they have unsuccessfully taught the first time. Therefore, it is critical that teachers understand that reteaching is not enlisting the same methodology (same method of input, same models, same procedure for checking for understanding), with the expectation that the results will change. It is, rather, a mandate to teach again, using other methods, models, materials, and so on. Therefore, we will include this step in our new model as well.

In the LaCroix model, the twelve critical steps involved in lesson planning are grouped together under three major headings: the Setup, the Lesson, and the Wrap-Up. Additionally, our format becomes circular, rather than linear, emphasizing the flexibility that must be inherent throughout our lesson and highlighting our belief that assessment and independent practice guide our steps as we begin to build our next lesson.

KEY RESOURCE 1.1

The LaCroix Model

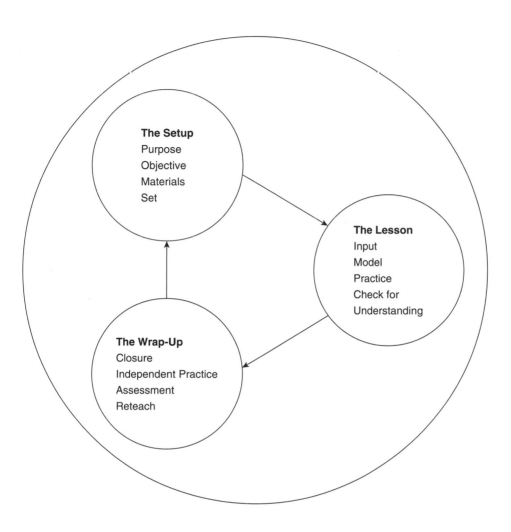

The Setup
Purpose
Objective
Materials
Set

The Lesson
Input
Model
Practice
Check for
Understanding

The Wrap-Up
Closure
Independent Practice
Assessment
Reteach

The Design 2

To find the journey's end in every step of the road . . .

Ralph Waldo Emerson

Having established a format for the lessons, we now turn our attention to unit design. This plan establishes the guiding philosophies and objectives from which our lessons will be drawn.

THE PURPOSE

Our purpose is multifaceted; at its core, it is our intent to give students the ability to read closely and understand fiction and poetry at a high level, a level at which they will be able to identify and explore the dilemma of the human condition. Our intent is to guide them through this process, with the expectation that they will draw conclusions, forming their own view of the world and their place in it. On an even loftier level, our purpose in teaching these units is to give them the gift of sight. It is not unlike the young sparrow that was born with vision in one eye and then has vision miraculously restored in his other eye; he views his world much differently now. It is the same world, but the sky appears bluer somehow, his mother's face more dear, and the far-off places to which he could only dream of soaring now are real possibilities. It is a slight difference, and yet it holds the possibility of being so much more.

THE OBJECTIVE

Our objective is to teach students how to read, interpret, present, and write about fiction and poetry.

THE CRUCIAL SETUP

The Anticipatory Set

How are we going to hook our students, to incite them to read and write about literature and poetry?

We will read short stories and poetry together. We will allow our students to choose the stories and poetry that speaks to them. We will surround them with powerful words that invoke powerful images. We will study the lives of the great bards and enlist the class historians as we discover together the poet in the poetry. We will tap into the students' interest in music and connect the rhythm and lyrics in song to the meter, rhyme, and beautiful language in poems. We will engage them in reading rich stories that prompt lively discussion. We will offer them tools by which they can unlock the meaning behind the meaning. We will lead them to understand that to read and appreciate great works of fiction is to live and appreciate life itself. We will openly celebrate their successes and gently correct their mistakes. Little by little, lesson by lesson, we are prepared to be as diligent and patient as necessary.

THE CRITICAL MATERIALS

The final step we must take to complete The Setup of our unit is to compile a list and either create or gather together all the materials we need. In a very basic unit, you will need the following:

Syllabus

Notebooks (poetry only)

Books (poetry only)

Posters/other visuals

Teaching poems

Short fiction selections

Worksheets

Rubrics/scoring guides

Tests and quizzes

The Syllabus

Let's begin with the syllabus. Some of you may be eliminating this step right away. After all, you prepared and sent home a syllabus the first week of school, and to send one again at the beginning of each unit seems redundant and time-consuming. I have found, however, that it is well worth our time and effort for a number of reasons.

Consider the time factor first. After you have read this book, or even this chapter, you will have gained enough understanding to rough out and prepare a syllabus for your first unit. If you are a beginning teacher, you may want to follow the format suggested at the end of this chapter, and if you are a veteran teacher who is looking to improve the unit you currently have in place, you can take what appeals to you, what you think may work well in your classes, and leave the rest. Either way, we are looking at a relatively small amount of time.

And what about effort? I understand that teachers are absolutely bombarded, on a daily basis, with items that require their attention and effort. There are the benchmark reading scores the facilitator needs by Friday, the three parent phones calls you need to return by the end of the day, the copying you must have ready for sixth period, and we could go on and on.

Regardless of the overwhelming demands on your time, the effort spent writing and distributing this syllabus warrants your attention. In the long run, it will save you time answering questions from students, parents, and administrators. Minimally and more precisely, it will clearly state your objective and purpose, detail the student's role and responsibility, and clarify the grading policy attached to the unit. Additionally, and as a bonus and natural by-product of creating and distributing a unit syllabus, you will maintain a clear picture of the objective, avoiding time-consuming pitfalls, maximizing the number of instructional minutes on task, and dramatically increasing the possibility of student success.

I strongly suggest that you write the syllabus in conjunction with your students (allowing them some input). Keep it to a maximum length of one page, and use the open-letter format printed on school or district letterhead (so that you can use the same document for multiple purposes and not have to reinvent the wheel each time). It's also a good idea to attain the principal's initials (approval) before distributing the document.

See an example of a poetry unit syllabus at the end of this chapter (Key Resource 2.1).

The Notebooks (Poetry Only)

I require that each student have a soft cover notebook to hold the many handouts that will be included in this unit. The purpose of the notebook is twofold. First, it assists the students in organizing their work. Second, the notebook can be reorganized, and, with the addition of a table of contents, it can serve as the student's culminating project.

It is critical that each student have a separate notebook for this unit because a percentage of their grade may be based on the notebook. No two notebooks will be alike. They will all choose different poems to present in the Friday poetry circles, they will all respond to the poems you discuss in class in a different way, and certainly they will all write poems that are uniquely their own.

The notebook, I explain to my students, is really a gift to them. I want them to pull this notebook out of a cedar chest when they are packing for college, or out of a box in their garage when they are married with their own children, and remember this time. I want the poetry book to be a collage of their feelings, their dreams, and their hopes when they were thirteen, fourteen, or fifteen years old.

Inevitably there will be students who do not procure a notebook. I simply buy a couple of packages of them, keep them at my desk, and sell them at cost (25 cents each if you get them on sale).

The Books (Poetry Only)

Next, you will need books, and you will need lots of them. You will need collections based on the works of one poet, collections based on themes, poetry collections that appeal to the very young and the very old. You will need books on poetry written centuries ago and books on poetry written last year. You will also need biographies and autobiographies, based on the lives of poets. You will need "how to" books—how to read poetry, how to analyze and interpret poetry, how to present poetry, how to identify the elements of poetry, and how to write poetry. The list could go on.

There are really only two criteria for judging books to be appropriate. First, they must be written in good taste and suitable for middle or high school readers. Second, they should not be nursery rhymes, used in the primary grades, or the simplistic or quirky poetry that are so appealing to the intermediate student. These books are absolutely wonderful and, if read well, have provided the secondary student with a sound foundation in the basics of the genre. I love these collections as well and have spent many nights reading them with my own children. However, if we do not force our middle school students to experience a new level of poetry, they never will. They may grumble, but my experience is that their discontent is short-lived. Within a few weeks, the students who complained the most become avid readers and vocal fans of Langston Hughes or Edgar Allan Poe or (surprisingly enough) even Emily Dickinson.

I'm going to make the assumption that the average teacher reading this book does not have an unlimited amount of school or personal funds (if any at all) to bankroll a collection this extensive. So here are a few options:

- Find out if there is money available in the school budget for classroom books.

- Visit your school's book room. (You may be surprised by the treasure trove of books you'll find here, stacked on shelves and waiting to be used.)

- Elicit the help of your school's PTA. (They may have funds and be willing to make a contribution, or they may be willing to raise the needed funds.)

- Plead your case at a faculty meeting. (Very often your fellow teachers have books that they will donate or lend.)

- Visit thrift stores, used book stores, library fundraising sales, and garage sales. (You can often find great collections for very little. Visit thrift stores often; remember that many have a daily turnover.)

- Ask your students and their parents for contributions. (Parents will often have poetry books from their high school or college years that have been stored in the garage and can prove invaluable when teaching the unit. Of course, you can always give them the opportunity to make a cash donation toward the class unit, as well.)

- Enlist the help of your school and local public librarians. (Explain the scope of your unit and ask how they might assist you in your endeavor. At the very minimum, they will allow you to check out the maximum number of books. Often, they will be willing to contribute out-dated editions.)

- Go to your local bookstore and find out if they would be willing to join you in this endeavor. (Many of the larger chains offer classroom teachers discounts. Often you can procure a number of books free in return for a public acknowledgment of their gift. These stores are often willing to provide a setting for a public display of student work or a poetry recital. More information on recitals is included in Chapter 5.)

- Create and execute a fundraising event, specifically for the purpose of raising money for books, with your students. (There are hundreds of ways to fund raise, and the experience is often a memorable one for your students.)

Here is a word to the wise about these solicitations. Keep your PTA informed and involved with your work toward building a class library. Often, PTAs have already enlisted the support of local merchants and have preplanned fundraisers. They have traditionally been the financial backbone of the school, the entity that provides extra materials, field trips, and other peak activities beyond the standard classroom experience. Align your efforts with theirs.

In addition, keep your principal informed about the nature of your activities. Calls may come into the office, and the principal and his or her staff need to have a clear idea of how to answer the question or to refer the inquiry to you. It is also important that the principal be informed because he or she may have a broader view of the school and its relationship with the community.

The Posters and Other Visuals

A great classroom starts with a great environment. Teachers have realized the importance of "setting the stage" for years. They don't report to their school sites, sometimes as much as a week before school (and their paycheck) starts, to prepare their classrooms because they have nothing better to do. They don't visit school suppliers and spend their hard-earned money on posters, charts, and other classroom visuals because they have unlimited funds. They don't visit other classrooms and talk with other teachers about their creative ideas for creating a motivating environment just because they enjoy the chitchat (although that certainly is part of it). They invest valuable time, money, and energy in this task, because they know it will reap great benefits during the school year. These teachers understand that first impressions are lasting impressions and that perception is reality. So their rooms take on themes reflecting the grade level and the subject taught.

Accordingly, a great classroom begins with a great environment, and a great environment requires time, money (resources), and energy. Primary teachers who work in self-contained classrooms have a clear disadvantage; given no aides or parent volunteers, they must invest their own time, money, and energy. Secondary teachers, on the other hand, have a clear advantage; given no aides or parent volunteers, they still have a valuable source of time, resources, and energy: the students in their classrooms.

Enlisting the talents and corralling the energy of your students to create a great classroom environment will produce five results:

1. It will relieve you of the burden of investing your own time, money, and energy.

2. It will build community among your students.

3. It will promote your students' sense of ownership.

4. It will provide avenues for self-expression.

5. It will produce a result that far exceeded your initial expectation.

Certainly, this approach can be considered a win–win solution for students and teachers. And it is not a difficult approach to put into action. Here are a few suggestions:

First, explain the scope of unit. If you have followed my earlier suggestion and have written a unit syllabus, then this step has already been achieved.

Second, gather ideas and make a plan. Include your ideas as well as your students' ideas and make a decision that includes some part of their input.

Third, gather materials. This will vary from classroom to classroom and unit to unit. It may include having rolls of butcher paper, broad-tipped markers, staplers, scissors, tape, and myriad other supplies. Additionally, the plan may call for artwork or other visuals produced by the students or materials brought to the school from other sources, such as paper bags from the local supermarket or wall border from a community retailer. (You can use your generic syllabus for this purpose as well. Businesses are often willing to extend a discount or donate the items you need.) Caution: Have all the materials ready before moving to the next step.

Fourth, execute the plan and decorate the room. This is where your management skills will be put to the test. Even with the proverbial best-laid plan, there is going to be a certain amount of chaos, but your goal will be to decorate the room with as little of this as possible. You might consider having one period (class) at a time be responsible for the entire room and rotate the task as you move from unit to unit. Another idea is to have different classes responsible for different areas of the room (e.g., Period 1 is assigned the SW corner, and Period 2 is assigned the NE corner; Period 3 puts up the backdrop, and Period 4 puts up the border).

Fifth, make sure everyone has a job (related to the decorating or academics) and give the students a limited amount of time. Regardless of the logistics of your plan, you want to make sure that each individual has something to do and that the students fully understand they have a limited amount of time to get the job done. Remember, students have no incentive to save you time. If you give them two hours, they will take every minute. If you give them one hour, they will complete the task in one hour. With the proper preparation (all materials and tools to complete the job are in place, and your students have a clear plan), this task can usually be completed in a reasonable amount of time. A good way to motivate students to produce their best work in a limited amount of time is to hold a contest, either among groups in the same class or among different classes.

One added word of advice: Always leave room for student work displays. You might designate a section of the wall be reserved for this purpose and have the paper or border changed as the units rotate.

The Teaching Poems

For the purpose of this unit, we consider "handouts" to be copies of poems that you will hand out to the entire class as you teach the conventions of poetry.

Some of these poems will serve as models of the Shakespearean sonnet, others will serve as examples of extended metaphors, and so on. You must have more than one poem that reflects a specific element in poetry. If you are teaching personification, for instance, one poem that contains this specific poetic device is far from adequate. The accomplished teacher of poetry teaches a concept, shows (models) many examples, uses other examples to check for understanding, uses still more for guided and independent practice, and possibly uses another one or two as an assessment tool. There is no question that these teaching poems will be essential to the success of your unit. Teaching poetry without poems might be compared to an attempt to describe the sky without using the color blue.

- Some poems will be included in your list of handouts because they offer rich material, language that stimulates your students sensibilities and lends itself to energetic class discussions.

- Some poems will be included because they have withstood the test of time and in so doing have come to be a part of the very fiber of the study of the genre.

- Some poems will be included because they are signature pieces of the great poets.

- Some poems will be included because you love them, because they speak to your passions.

- And still others will be included because your students love them, because they speak to their passions.

At the end of this chapter I have included a listing of poems that may serve as seed for your poetry unit. These are simply poems that I have found to be consistently popular with students. When you teach to a specific poem, make sure that all students (for some of you reading this book, that may well mean

180 copies) are given a copy of the poem to be included in their individual poetry books.

You can prepare beforehand by having a number of these poems copied and ready for distribution. Other poems, those that most certainly will be shared in class discussions or presented during the weekly circles, will need to be copied and distributed as they are shared. (I discuss the culminating activities in more depth in Chapter 5.)

Although you should certainly have the copies ready for distribution to your classes, do not make the mistake of handing them all out at the beginning of the unit. These poems should be distributed to the class at the same time they are being addressed in a particular lesson. With this format, students are more likely to take on an active, rather than a passive, learning role. This study is meant to be a cooperative effort, a joint undertaking by the students and teacher. Although well planned, the unit will and should take on a design of its own. I referred to every poem that I passed out to my students during this unit as a present for them. They may very well have groaned each time they entered my class and I told them that I had two (!) presents for them that day, but they groaned with a smile. In return, I genuinely thanked them when they brought in a poem that spoke to me.

The poems I have included on my list at the end of this chapter evolved over the course of a number of years. They will help you to organize your first unit. I encourage you to add to the list, including especially those poems that appeal to you. Remember that your enthusiasm is absolutely necessary to the success of this unit. So, teach what you love. Additionally, and on a more practical level, keep in mind that you will require a number of examples when teaching poetic devices. Poems are like diamonds—you can never have too many.

The Short Fiction Selections

In the lessons provided in Chapter 4, I have provided short fiction pieces to use as the initial model for the strategy or skill being taught. It will be necessary for the classroom teacher to research the resources in her room or at her site that will serve as other rich examples. Excerpts from novels can also be used. In this case, the text may prompt students to read the full text.

The Worksheets

In Chapter 4, I refer to a number of worksheets I devised for my students' use when teaching short fiction and poetry. Primarily, I used worksheets when teaching a specific element of the genre, or when I was attempting to jump-start the creative juices needed to write a response to literature.

The inclusion of these tools should not be perceived as an endorsement of any one instructional methodology. I used a variety of teaching strategies in my classroom. The use of a worksheet was just one of many tools I enlisted in my craft.

You may want to consider some of the examples of worksheets presented in Chapter 4, make your own, or borrow them from another teacher. Regardless of your approach, you still need to plan ahead and duplicate those that you feel you are most apt to use.

The Rubrics and Scoring Guides

Rubrics (also referred to as scoring guides) are critical to the success of a unit. There is no one way to develop a rubric. It is essential, however, that you establish the rubrics needed prior to teaching a unit. Like the syllabus, it will define and clarify, for you and for your students, the model end result. This end result could be, for example, a writing assignment, a dramatic reading, or a poetry notebook.

Nothing will do more to support your efforts in the classroom than the use of a rubric. A rubric does much to level the playing field by presenting a clear picture of the desired outcome. Students simply cannot be successful, or even be held accountable for their efforts, unless they have this clarity.

On the other hand, rubrics must allow for a subjective judgment of student work. There is no question that most English assignments must be graded somewhat subjectively. As teachers of language, we must have the flexibility, the ability to raise or lower a grade based on the rhetorical effectiveness of the writing. We must reserve some license to break with convention from time to time—in this case the rubric or scoring guide—and reward or mark down a student's writing based on its rhetorical merit.

Consequently, a rubric needs to be prepared (with student input when warranted) thoughtfully and carefully. It must clearly spell out the objective and set a standard in an effort to grade students fairly based on a shared vision of what delineates proficient from nonproficient work. At the same time, it must allow for some subjective evaluation on the part of the teacher. Often this is accomplished by writing a clear, objective rubric (almost a checklist), and adding into each score qualitative verbiage such as "insightful," "thorough," "underdeveloped," "adequate," "stimulating," "lacks details," "creative," "satisfactory," "unsatisfactory," "proficient," and "poor."

I have never encountered two rubrics that are exactly alike, but they all share at least one quality. In every rubric, a number (designating the quality of the work) or a letter grade (A–F) is used in a linear fashion, with the highest grade or number representing the highest quality work. I have used 4-point and 6-point rubrics with success.

With a simple 4-point rubric, levels 1 and 2 are not proficient and levels 3 and 4 are proficient. A 4-point rubric is easier to score; you draw a general opinion regarding the overall proficiency level (i.e., is it or is it not proficient?). After making this initial (general) assessment, you consider the work again and determine between a score ½ or a score ¾, based on the finer qualities of the work. A 4-point rubric is also useful when attempting to transfer the rubric score into a letter grade (A/4, B/3, C/2, D/1). In this scoring format, a score of 2 would represent a passing (C) grade. A sample 4-point rubric follows this chapter (Key Resource 2.3).

I am acquainted with several teachers who prefer the 6-point rubric because it makes allowances for those papers that fall between the lines of a

4-point rubric. With this format you can reward the student who works hard and hands in strong work (score of 5) but whose writing consistently lacks what I call "star quality," that indefinable something that is essential to a 6 score. A score of 6 is rare in my class because the 6 is reserved for those writings that clearly go well beyond my expectations and often offer a unique perspective. Additionally, a 6 score at this high level of expectation continually challenges your more talented writers and raises the standard for all your students.

Another benefit of the 6-point rubric is that it allows a degree of acknowledgment to the student who has made some effort (score of 2) and the student who has clearly put forth no effort (score of 1).

When using a 6-point rubric, clearly explain to your classes how their rubric score would translate into a letter grade. I have visited classrooms in which a 3 was passing and others where a 4 was passing. Consider which system would most likely meet the needs of your classes, draw that line of demarcation, and remain consistent as you move from assignment to assignment. A sample 6-point rubric follows this chapter (Key Resource 2.4).

Make the decision about which rubric will work best in your classroom and stick with that decision. Each type of rubric has its merits. Decide which rubric will work best in your classroom, and consistently use the same type (4 or 6 point). If you move back and forth, between a 6- and 4-point rubric, students will likely become confused. Increased confusion produces decreased motivation. Spend time "teaching" the rubric at the beginning of the year or the beginning of the unit, remain consistent, and then move to your content. New content (and much of what you will be teaching is new content) should be presented in a familiar structure to ensure maximum retention. Never present a new idea when introducing a new format; it may well be a recipe for failure.

Finally, I would caution you about using a rubric for every assignment. The great majority of student work that occurs in the classroom should be in the form of practice. Students must have the opportunity to work with the material, as the teacher gradually releases the responsibility of mastery on to the student. This whole idea of practice speaks to the very heart of teaching.

The Tests and Quizzes

I still believe that tests and quizzes have their place and serve a purpose in the classroom. This certainly should not be your only assessment tool, but it should be included for a number of reasons. One benefit of a test is that it can be designed to be totally objective, and objective tests can usually be graded fairly and quickly, offering your students immediate feedback. Nothing will do more to motivate a student than knowledge of results, and tests will provide this. Second (and this is a huge plus), tests often raise the students' level of concern; if they understand that they are going to be held accountable for the content, they generally are going to be more attentive and diligent. Finally, regardless of the content we teach, each teacher is preparing his or her students for the real world, and in the real world there are tests. Our students need the opportunity to study, to access information, and to discover how they learn best. Considering the rate at which the worlds' knowledge base is growing, not to teach them this skill, not to allow them this opportunity, would be a disservice.

I also believe that tests should be fair and present no less and no more than the content covered. I may use tests used in previous years as models, but they are never exactly alike. It isn't that I enjoy writing new assessments each year, it is simply that I don't teach the same content each year. For instance, even if I am using the same poems, teaching the same devices, and using the same notes, no class is every exactly the same. In one class, a discussion about the life of Edgar Allan Poe may have generated a lot of discussion. Because of those "teachable moments," the lesson took three days rather than two, and we covered a great deal more information than I had with the previous year's class. Consequently, the quiz I administer based on this information will contain more on Poe than did the previous year's assessment. I generally quiz on the same day each week (Thursdays) and base that test on the material covered in class since the previous weekly test.

With a sound design in place, we are now ready to teach the foundational lessons.

KEY RESOURCE 2.1

Sample Syllabus

To: Parent, Administrator, etc.   Date _____
From: Your name and title
Re: Name of your poetry unit

Dear_____,

(Objective)
Over the course of the next several weeks, our class will be studying poetry.
We will be

reading and identifying the unique elements of the genre.

offering dramatic oral presentations of poetry.

writing our own verse.

(Purpose)
In so doing, it is our hope that we will gain a deeper understanding of
language and become better readers, writers, and speakers.

(Student Responsibilities)
On a weekly basis, we will

read and analyze poetry.

identify figurative language used in poetry.

present dramatic readings of poetry.

discuss how language contributes to the poem's effect.

study the lives of great poets.

write our own poems.

At the end of the unit we will

publish individual poetry books, chronicling our work in this unit.

participate in a poetry recital (to which you will be invited).

(Grading)
Students will be graded according to the following formula:

Ongoing: Culminating:
40% Classwork   15% Poetry book
10% Homework assignments   15% Poetry recital
10% Participation in weekly poetry circles
10% Tests and quizzes

Sincerely,
Mrs. LaCroix and the Class of Room 103 (Principal's Initials)

KEY RESOURCE 2.2

Teaching Poems

Poems About Poetry

* "The Day Is Done"	Henry Wadsworth Longfellow
"Feelings About Words"	Mary O'Neill
"Imagination" (from *A Midsummer Night's Dream*)	William Shakespeare
"Poetry Should Ride the Bus"	Ruth Forman
"Proud Words"	Carl Sandburg

Poems That Teach Lessons

* "If Tomorrow Never Comes"	Anonymous
"Into the Sun"	Hannah Kahn
* "O Great Spirit"	Anonymous
* "Ode: Intimations of Immortality"	William Wordsworth
* "The Psalm of Life"	Henry Wadsworth Longfellow
* "To be, or not to be" (from *Hamlet*)	William Shakespeare
* "To thine own self be true" (from *Hamlet*)	William Shakespeare
* "The Village Blacksmith"	Henry Wadsworth Longfellow

High Interest Poems

"Always Hold On to Your Dreams"	Nancye Sims
"Be Nobody's Darling"	Alice Walker
"Comes the Dawn"	V.A. Shoffstall
"If I Were in Charge of the World"	Judith Viorst

Examples of Alliteration

"Fire and Ice"	Robert Frost
"I Never Saw a Moor"	Emily Dickinson
"Sir Gawain and the Green Knight"	Anonymous
"Success Is Counted Sweetest"	Emily Dickinson
* "The Village Blacksmith"	Henry Wadsworth Longfellow

Example of Free Verse

"Ode to Mi Gato"	Gary Soto

Image Poems

"Fog"	Carl Sandburg
"Into the Sun"	Hannah Kahn
"Oranges"	Gary Soto
"The Road Not Taken"	Robert Frost

*These poems are included in the lessons in Chapter Four.

"Steam Shovel"	Charles Malam
"Stopping by Woods on a Snowy Evening"	Robert Frost
"Waiting on Summer"	Ruth Forman

Examples of Metaphors

* "All the world's a stage" (from *As You Like It*)	William Shakespeare
"Dreams"	Langston Hughes
"Fog"	Carl Sandburg
"Giraffes"	Sy Kahn
"He Jests at Scars" (from *Romeo and Juliet*)	William Shakespeare
"A Narrow Fellow in the Grass"	Emily Dickinson
"The Pheasant"	Robert P. Tristram Coffin
"Steam Shovel"	Charles Malam
"Success Is Counted Sweetest"	Emily Dickinson
"The Toaster"	William Jay Smith

Narrative Verse

* "Annabel Lee"	Edgar Allan Poe
"Casey at the Bat"	Ernest L. Thayer
"Oranges"	Gary Soto
"Sir Gawain and the Green Knight"	Anonymous
"The Trouble Was Meals"	Elizabeth Bennett

Examples of Personification

* "A Split Tree Still Grows"	Anonymous
"Barter"	Sara Teasdale
* "Because I Could Not Stop for Death"	Emily Dickinson
"He Jests at Scars" (from *Romeo and Juliet*)	William Shakespeare
"I Wandered Lonely as a Cloud"	William Wordsworth
* "Like as the Waves"	William Shakespeare
"Lost"	Carl Sandburg
"March"	Solveig Paulson Russell
* "Nature, the Gentlest Mother"	Emily Dickinson
"On the Pulse of Morning"	Maya Angelou

Examples of Similes

* "All the world's a stage" (from *As You Like It*)	William Shakespeare
"Giraffes"	Sy Kahn
* "Like as the Waves"	William Shakespeare
"A Narrow Fellow in the Grass"	Emily Dickinson
* "To Helen"	Edgar Allan Poe
* "The Village Blacksmith"	Henry Wadsworth Longfellow

*These poems are included in the lessons in Chapter Four.

KEY RESOURCE 2.3

Chaser Poem Rubric (4 Point)

To score a 4, your writing will

_____ be complete and grammatically correct.

_____ include elevated vocabulary that coincides with the rhythm of the original poem.

_____ develop and maintain a new, central focus, based on the marriage of the lines.

_____ be engaging, creative, and thoughtful.

To score a 3, your writing will

_____ be complete and contain few grammatical errors.

_____ include elevated vocabulary.

_____ add to the effect of the original poem, maintaining a well-controlled awareness of the emerging poem.

_____ be thoughtful and generally competent.

To score a 2, your writing will

_____ be somewhat complete, but contain many errors.

_____ include basic vocabulary.

_____ mirror the intent of the original poem.

_____ offer little elaboration.

To score a 1, your writing will

_____ be incomplete and riddled with errors.

_____ include simple vocabulary and may be illogical.

_____ do little to further the intent of the original poem.

_____ be brief and possibly incoherent.

KEY RESOURCE 2.4

Bio Poem Rubric (6 Point)

To score a 6, your writing will

_____ be complete, grammatically correct, and contain descriptive phrases in lines 3 through 9.

_____ have a creative title that immediately engages the reader.

_____ vividly re-create the subject.

_____ describe fully and offer examples of personal associations/taste.

_____ use sensory details, specific actions, and/or dialogue to help the reader visualize the subject.

_____ use a variety of rhetorical structures and language to convey purpose, direction, and movement.

_____ be fresh, creative, and original.

To score a 5, your writing will

_____ be complete, grammatically correct, and contain descriptive phrases in lines 3 through 9.

_____ have a creative title.

_____ clearly define or identify the subject.

_____ describe and offer examples of personal associations/taste.

_____ include enough detail to re-create the subject.

_____ use some variety of rhetorical devices.

_____ be interesting and enthusiastic.

To score a 4, your writing will

_____ be complete, grammatically correct, and contain some phrases.

_____ have an interesting title.

_____ clearly define or identify the subject.

_____ describe some personal associations/taste.

_____ use some details to begin to create an impression about the subject.

_____ use too much or too little information.

_____ be predictable, but still strong.

To score a 3, your writing will

_____ be complete, contain few grammatical errors, and some phrases in lines 3 through 9.

_____ have a general title that states subject's name or Bio Poem.

_____ identify the subject.

_____ state personal associations/taste.

_____ contain few details/often a listing.

_____ offer too much information about the subject or leave out important information.

_____ be predictable and shallow.

To score a 2, your writing will

_____ not be fully complete and contain several grammatical errors.

_____ may or may not contain a title.

_____ state the subject.

_____ reveal minimal personal associations/taste.

_____ contain only general, scanty information/often a listing.

To score a 1, your writing will

_____ be incomplete.

_____ provide little or no information about the subject.

The Preparation 3

A man should ever, as much as in him lieth,
be ready booted to take his journey.

Michel de Montaigne

SKILLS TO BE TAUGHT

Now that we have clarified our purpose and written a broad objective, it is necessary (1) to detail what skills will need to be taught and (2) to design a specific plan of action, day-to-day lesson plans that will enable us to reach that objective.

As a starting point, we return to our unit objective, to teach students how to read, interpret, write, and present poetry and fiction.

Next, we will list the skills that must be taught to achieve this objective:

I. If we are going to teach students how to read poetry, we must teach
   - the value of multiple readings
   - the significance of punctuation/capitalization
   - the importance of word choice
   - the impact of rhyme and meter

II. If we are going to teach students how to read literature, we must teach
   - that meaning is constructed as we read
   - that the individual's experience with text is uniquely one's own
   - how to ask critical questions that lead to greater understanding
   - that literature that rewards close reading is literature that speaks to the dilemma of the human condition

III. If we are going to teach students how to interpret poetry, we must teach
   - rhyme scheme and rhyme deviation
   - various types of poetry (e.g., narrative, sonnet)
   - symbolism, similes, metaphors, onomatopoeia, alliteration, and so on
   - how the poem reflects the poet

IV. If we are going to teach students how to analyze literature, we must teach
- how an author's style contributes to the work
- the role of conflict and resolution
- identification of the deeper framework of the text
- characterization and its association with the major themes of the work

V. If we are going to teach students how to write poetry, we must teach
- the great significance of word choice
- the structure of poetry (e.g., line, stanza)
- the benefit of incorporating specific and descriptive language
- the various formats that can be used to create poems

VI. If we are going to teach students how to write about fiction, we must teach
- the conventions of standard English
- clear, coherent, and compelling written communication skills
- persuasive writing techniques
- the necessity of justifying assertions with textual evidence

VII. If we are going to teach students how to present publicly, we must teach
- the correlation between voice clarity and posture
- the importance of maintaining eye contact
- the use of dramatic pauses
- the power of body language and voice inflection

Now that the skills have been itemized, our task is to write specific lesson plans that correlate with these skills while integrating a broad sampling of poetry and fiction.

The planning and the execution of the elements of the lesson (input, model, practice, and checking for understanding) are what separate true teaching professionals from the laypersons. Individuals who are new to teaching can generally establish (albeit often broadly) an objective and purpose and gather together materials.

What often takes years to refine, however, is the process of disseminating the content (input), showing or demonstrating what the task looks like (modeling), allowing learners adequate time to work with the material (practice), and, the most critical decision of all, determining whether the learners have mastered the content to the extent that they are ready to move on to the next chunk of content (checking for understanding).

The Wrap-Up is also essential to the lesson. If, at the end of a lesson, the teacher has determined that sufficient learning has not taken place, she returns to the drawing board and creates a new lesson (may change method of input, increase number of models, spend more time with students as they practice application of the content). Closure provides learners with an opportunity to file the new information mentally (so that they may retrieve it). It may also offer students an opportunity to practice the new skill or apply the new content on their own (independent practice). In addition, the Wrap-Up factors in assessment, which in itself also serves as a check for understanding and helps the professional to determine whether reteaching is necessary.

Equipped with this knowledge, we are now prepared to move on to planning the specific lessons, which will enable us to achieve our goals. For practical purposes, I have created the lessons based on the LaCroix model.

Poetry Only: Before you begin to teach the poetry unit, there are two procedural lessons that must precede the academic lessons in Chapter 4. Together, they provide the backbone of the unit: the poetry notebook and the dramatic reading requirements.

PROCEDURAL LESSON 1: THE POETRY NOTEBOOK

I inform my students of the importance of keeping all their materials in their poetry notebooks and remind them that the notebook will serve two purposes: It will serve as a reflection of their work during the course of this unit, and it will aid me in the grading process.

Set: "Have you ever sat with your family and looked over old photographs, photos of you when you were a baby, when you had your fifth birthday, when you went to school for the first time, or when you lost your first tooth? How does it feel when you look at these pictures? Why is it important to try and capture the moments of our past?" Class discusses.

Purpose: "Over the course of the next few weeks, you (students) will be involved in a process of capturing this moment in time. Rather than pictures, our new memory will be encapsulated in language."

Objective: "Rather than a photo album, our memory keeper will be a poetry book, a poetry book that will contain the poems we have discussed in class, as well as the poems you (students) personally have chosen or written because they are important to you."

Input: Teacher hands out and discusses notebook requirements. (See Poetry Book Requirement at the end of this chapter.)

Model: First year teaching the unit: I would advise that you put together a mock poetry book or your own poetry book (students may get to know a whole different side of you) that contains all the essential elements required. At the end of this first year, ask permission to make copies of individual books to serve as models for subsequent years. Next years teaching the unit: Pass around poetry books that you (with the students' permission) have copied to serve as models for future books. The students should see a number of books that represent quality work but that are at the same time decisively different. You want them to understand fully that accomplished work, for the purposes of this unit of study, can differ vastly in appearance.

Assessment: At the end of the unit.

PROCEDURAL LESSON 2: THE DRAMATIC READING

The second procedural lesson to be taught is vital to the students' ongoing success because each Friday they will be held accountable for their efforts in this area. On this day, students participate in a class Poetry Circle and are required to offer a dramatic rendering of a poem not under study in the class. Our second task, therefore, focuses on the presentation of a poem.

Set: Stand before the class, and with no introductory remarks, offer a poor reading of a poem. Allow the paper on which the poem is printed to somewhat obstruct your voice. Slouch, pay no attention to the poem's punctuation, occasionally mispronounce a word, and make sure that your voice is mundane and bland. Ask students what they thought the poem was about. How did it make them feel? What are their thoughts about the poem? Does the poem remind them of anything? What sort of person do you image the author to be? (They should find it hard to answer these questions.) Then, stand before the class with the same poem and offer a good example of the dramatic reading, using the same poem. Follow with the same questions. (They should be able to engage in some discussion at this point.) Then ask: "What were some of the differences between the first reading and the second?" Chart their answers.

Objective: "Today we will begin to understand how, simply by using a few practical suggestions, we can all make poetry come alive by reading it deliberately and with feeling and flair."

Purpose: "Some of you may be thinking: So what? I never intend to become a poet. Why should I care about making poetry come alive? Before you turn a silent ear, consider your life goals. Do you want to be a businessperson? A teacher? A coach? A salesman? A lawyer? A member of Congress? If the answer is yes, then you might reconsider. Poetry is simply the vehicle we are going to use to teach you how to communicate more clearly and how to stand before a group and speak effectively, two skills that are essential to success in any number of careers."

Input/Model: Dramatic reading rubric. (See sample at the end of the chapter.) Teacher discusses and models each element.

Practice/Checking for Understanding: Students are put into groups of three. Each group is given three poems (it's OK to use the same three poems with each group). Students are given rubrics to score each other. Individuals spend some time reading and practicing their poems and then perform before the other two members of their group, who score the reading according to the rubric. The process continues until all students have presented.

Checking for Understanding: Teacher moves from group to group, keeping students on task, offering suggestions, and making mental notes.

Independent Practice: Students are given a couple of days to choose a poem that they would like to present. I explain to them that there will be a time for writing and sharing their own pieces later in the unit but that I need them to use a published poet for their class presentation. Additionally, they are told that they are not to memorize the poem, but rather concentrate on the skills they need to bring to a dramatic reading to bring meaning to the poem. I require that students bring in their poems over the course of the next two days in order to have the material approved prior to the presentation. I use the following criteria when considering a poem for approval:

- Is the poem appropriate?

- Is the poem too short or too long? You want to ensure enough time, so that all students can present during the Friday Poetry Circle. If a student brings in a short poem by Emily Dickinson, I generally ask the student to add two or three more short selections by the author and present them all. If the poem is clearly too long, I may ask the student to present just the first and last stanzas, the first three stanzas, or another portion of it. My suggestion will differ, of course, depending on the poem and the student. By using this system, I am able to honor the student's choice and still reserve time so that all students have the opportunity to read.

- Is the poem one that the student can read and understand? I teach students that it is critical that they are able to pronounce and understand each word of the poem, and have drawn a conclusion regarding the poem's overall meaning. I explain to them that you cannot "bring meaning" to a poem through your presentation unless you have a sound understanding of it.

After they have received approval on their poem, students spend the next few days practicing. Initially, this practice may take place in the classroom and at home. In later weeks you may want them to practice exclusively at home in front of the mirror or in front of their families and friends. Regardless of where and when they practice, however, you must emphasize over and over again the importance of practice, practice, practice. You also need to emphasize that reading the poem silently over and over again is not considered valid practice for an oral presentation and will do nothing to improve their oral language skills. They must read the poem aloud, and they must use the rubric to check the quality of their presentation (e.g., Is my posture straight? Am I offering sufficient eye contact?).

Assessment: Assessment for the dramatic reading occurs each Friday over the course of the unit and is ongoing. On these days, the chairs and desks in the room are arranged in a circle. Students are seated alphabetically, according to last names, asked to put everything away except their poems, and to turn over the poems in their laps or on their desks. The students are arranged alphabetically because it assists me as I assess initially and later as I assess them based on their individual progress. I have them clear their desks and turn over their poems to eliminate possible distracters. I sit in the circle with my students with a clipboard that contains a number of rubrics separated by carbon paper; one rubric remains with me, and the carbon is passed on to the student at the end of the poetry circle. (See Key Resource 3.2, Dramatic Reading Rubric, and Key Resource 3.3, Poetry Circle Grade, at the end of this chapter.) I use this method of assessment for several reasons.

1. I am able to provide the students with immediate feedback on their presentations.

2. I am able to chart each student's progress.

3. I am able to apply a grade to my grade book.

Before the readings begin, I speak to the students about the absolute necessity of all students in the circle giving their complete, undivided attention to the person rendering the dramatic reading. I advise them of the great benefits to be gained through observing others. It is critical to the success of the poetry circles, and ultimately the success of the unit, that this high level of attention be maintained. Address even the slightest transgression and insist on compliance.

Each student begins by stating the title and author of the poem and the stanzas they will be reading from the poem (if applicable). I join my class in remaining silent and attentive during this time. After each student's reading, I take a few minutes to mark his or her rubric. I then offer that student a brief word of praise and a suggestion for improvement. Applause is held until all students have read. At the end of the period, or often at the end of the day, I give students the carbon copy of their rubric, which restates the praise and suggestion for improvement offered after the reading and which also contains a grade, or rubric score.

If a student does not have a poem prepared to read, I do not engage him or her in conversation nor do I reprimand. To maintain the integrity of the Poetry Circle, I simply make a quick note on my grading rubric and call on the next student.

If a student clearly has not prepared for the reading (you will know this right away) or is not taking the presentation seriously, I interrupt the reading and ask the student to sit down. Again, I do not engage the student in discussion; I make a quick note on my grading rubric and move on to the next student. There is no need for you to offer the student or the class a reason for your action. It will be clear to them as well.

You are now prepared and ready to teach your lessons.

KEY RESOURCE 3.1

Poetry Book Requirement

1. The front cover should include a visual, a creative title, and the author's name.

2. All materials must be three-hole punched and affixed to the notebook.

3. The book should contain

    a dedication page

    a table of contents

    poems and worksheets used in class

    poems written by the student

    poems analyzed by the student

    poems presented by the student

    a reflective journal

    a glossary of poetic terms

4. All pages should be

    numbered

    neat

    accurate

    complete

KEY RESOURCE 3.2

Dramatic Reading Rubric

6 – Excellent

_____ Excellent posture

_____ Consistent eye contact

_____ Projects voice well

_____ Uses body language

_____ Uses dramatic pauses

_____ Varies speed and volume of speech

5 – Good

_____ Good posture

_____ Consistent eye contact

_____ Projects voice fairly well

_____ Uses body language or dramatic pauses

_____ Varies speed or volume of speech

4 – Satisfactory

_____ Adequate posture

_____ Good eye contact

_____ Projects voice somewhat

_____ Use of one or more of the following:

Body language

Dramatic pauses

Varied speed or volume of speech

3 – Needs Improvement

_____ Poor posture

_____ Little eye contact

_____ Weak voice projection

_____ No body language, dramatic pauses, or varied speech

2 – Unsatisfactory

_____ Poor posture

_____ No eye contact

_____ Little voice projection

_____ No body language, dramatic pauses, or varied speech

1 – Unacceptable; read with no effort.

KEY RESOURCE 3.3

Poetry Circle Grade

Poetry Circle # _____

Name _____

Date _____

Poem _____

Rubric Grade _____

Good job _____

_____

Need to work on _____

_____

Poetry Circle # _____

Name _____

Date _____

Poem _____

Rubric Grade _____

Good job _____

_____

Need to work on _____

The Lessons 4

The soul of a journey is liberty, perfect liberty,
to think, feel, do just as one pleases.

William Hazlitt

LESSON 1

Understanding Character Through Tragedy

The Setup

Purpose:

To offer students an understanding and appreciation of a close examination of characterization in tragic short fiction.

Objective:

Students will write an essay that answers the following question: In the short story [*determined by teacher*], which characters were most responsible for the outcome of the story? In other words, which characters contributed to the story's tragic ending?

Materials Provided:

Worksheet: "Ladder of Responsibility"
Worksheet: "Literary Report Card"
Handout: "Summary of Characters in Shakespeare's *Hamlet*"
Essay Scoring Guide for Student Response to Literature

Materials to Be Collected:

A copy of the fairy tale "Little Red Riding Hood," with an altered ending (the grandmother dies)
A summary of Shakespeare's *Hamlet*
A rich short story with a tragic ending

Optional Materials:

Story: "Teenage Wasteland" by Anne Tyler
Poem: "The Wasteland" by T. S. Eliot
Song: "Teenage Wasteland" by The Who (1965)

Set:

Teacher offers students a number of story scenarios with tragic endings. They can make them up or even pull them from current events. Example: A young toddler wanders off into a neighbor's yard, finds the gate to the pool open, enters, falls in the pool, and drowns. Who is at fault? Is it the mother who should have been supervising the child more carefully or the neighbor who should have checked to be sure the gate was properly locked?

The Lesson

Input/Model/Check for Understanding/Practice:

Pass out "Ladder of Responsibility." Class reads together the story of "Little Red Riding Hood" with the altered ending. Students consider the demise of the grandmother. Who was responsible? Was it Little Red Riding Hood's mother? The wolf? The grandmother? Or was it Little Red Riding Hood herself? Was one character more responsible than the other? Students are then asked to write the characters' names on the "Ladder of Responsibility," placing the one they believe to be the most responsible on the highest rung of the ladder.

All of these questions are discussed with the class. Certainly, there will (and should) be more than one correct answer. All answers that can be supported by the text of the story are accepted. The only wrong answers are those that cannot be supported by the storyline or text.

Conclusion: Because we each interact with fictional text in different ways, it is likely that we will draw dissimilar conclusions regarding any story. And, it is very possible that there will be more than one "right answer." The only "wrong" answer is the one that cannot be supported by textual evidence. It may be helpful to use a courtroom analogy here: A court must decide who is responsible for the death of Granny. If one lawyer (student) is asserting that the main culprit is the wolf, that student is then asked for the specific evidence to back up the claim. In other words, pull those exact words from the text that support the claim. If there is no evidence, the claim is deemed inadmissible and thrown out of the courtroom.

Students read a summary of Shakespeare's *Hamlet.*

Teacher asks the class to consider the ending of this play using the "Ladder of Responsibility." The question: Who was most responsible for the tragic ending? (Summary of main characters may well be of use here.)

Students work in pairs and consider where they would place the characters on the ladder and to pull textual evidence from the text. Whole class discussion follows.

Students read a short story or play with a tragic ending (provided by the teacher). They list all the characters in the story and then write their names on the ladder, placing the character they determine to be the most responsible at the top of the ladder. The placement of each additional character on the ladder is also supported by textual evidence.

The Wrap-Up

Closure:

Students share their insights in regard to the last selection read.

Independent Practice:

Using the same story and a completed "Ladder of Responsibility," students write an essay supporting a thesis statement asserting that three characters in the story (as determined by the student) are most responsible for the tragic end.

Assessment:

Scoring Guide

Reteach:

If necessary.

Added Notes:

The story "Teenage Wasteland" by Anne Tyler would be an excellent story to use as independent practice. The song by the same title and recorded by The Who, as well as the poem by T. S. Eliot, "The Wasteland," can be used as sets or as companion pieces.

I have included another worksheet titled "Literary Report Card." This strategy, which asks students to "grade" characters under the subject headings of Courage, Wisdom, Loyalty, and Integrity, can also be used to prompt students to take a closer look at fictional characters. The comments section is used to provide textual evidence that supports the grades given. Other categories that might be included on the report card are Competency, Kindness, Responsibility, Communication Skills, Empathy, and Creativity.

KEY RESOURCE 4.1

Ladder of Responsibility

KEY RESOURCE 4.2

Summary of Characters in Shakespeare's Hamlet

King Hamlet

The deceased king of Denmark and father of Hamlet, prince of Denmark.

Claudius

The new king of Denmark who murdered his brother, King Hamlet, and married his sister-in-law, Queen Gertrude. Claudius sends Hamlet (the prince of Denmark) to England with orders that Hamlet should be killed. When that plan fails, he arranges a duel between Hamlet and Laertes, ensuring the death of Hamlet by poisoning the tip of Laertes' sword and Hamlet's victory cup—in case Hamlet wins. Hamlet fatally stabs Claudius in the last scene.

Gertrude

Married to the king of Denmark and then to Claudius, she tries to reason with Hamlet to stop his campaign against Claudius. In the last scene, she drinks from the poisoned cup intended for Hamlet and dies.

Polonius

Advisor to Claudius, who spies on Hamlet and in the process is mistaken for Claudius and killed by Hamlet.

Ophelia

Polonius' daughter, who becomes a pawn in Hamlet's scheme to seek revenge on Claudius. Driven to madness by her father's death, she throws herself in a stream and dies.

Laertes

Polonius' son who, enraged over the deaths of his father and sister, engages Hamlet in a duel. He is killed in the duel by the end of the poisoned sword intended for Hamlet.

Hamlet

The son of the deceased King Hamlet and Queen Gertrude, the prince of Denmark, enraged over his father's death at the hand of Claudius, plots revenge. He dies in the duel with Laertes by the same poisoned sword.

Horatio

Hamlet's friend who assists in bringing Hamlet to see his father's ghost and who lives to tell of the story of King Hamlet's death.

KEY RESOURCE 4.3

Essay Scoring Guide for Student Response to Literature

Not Evident				Very Evident
0	1	2	3	4

0	1	2	3	4	Does the introduction to the essay engage the reader's attention?
0	1	2	3	4	Does the introduction clearly state the purpose of the writing?
0	1	2	3	4	Does the introduction include the title and author of the text to be discussed?
0	1	2	3	4	Does the writer organize the essay into well-developed paragraphs?
0	1	2	3	4	Does the writer fully develop insights about the text that reflect careful reading and understanding?
0	1	2	3	4	Does the writer justify his or her insights by citing examples or textual evidence?
0	1	2	3	4	Does the writer use effective transitions?
0	1	2	3	4	Does the writer use elevated vocabulary and a variety of sentence structures?
0	1	2	3	4	Does the writer draw the essay to a natural conclusion?
0	1	2	3	4	Is the essay well crafted and free of grammatical errors?

KEY RESOURCE 4.4

Literary Report Card

Name of Character: _____

Subject	Grade	Comment
Courage		_____ _____ _____ _____
Wisdom		_____ _____ _____ _____
Loyalty		_____ _____ _____ _____
Integrity		_____ _____ _____ _____

LESSON 2

Conflict and the Heroic Journey

The Setup

Purpose:

To offer students an understanding and appreciation of the framework of the heroic journey and the role of conflict in short fiction.

Objective:

Students will identify the heroic journey and the conflict that perpetuates that journey in three self-selected short stories; students will identify the heroic journey in a short story and write an essay based on those findings; or they can undertake both objectives.

Materials Provided:

Story: "Miracle on the Bayou" by Lorraine LaCroix
Worksheet: "The Heroic Journey"
Essay Scoring Guide (Key Resource 4.3 from Lesson 1)

Materials to Be Collected:

A number of children's books/stories that serve as good examples of the journey motif.
(Example: "The Little Boy Who Cried Wolf")
Selections of young adult stories that also serve as good examples of the motif.

Optional Materials:

Poem: "After a While" by Virginia Shoffstall
Short story: "A Boy and His Dog" by Martha Brooks
Excerpt from novel: *A Day No Pigs Would Die* by Newton Peck
(when young protagonist watches his father slaughter a pig)
Selected excerpts from films and television to serve as additional models.

Set:

How many of you once believed in Santa Claus? Did you ever believe in the Tooth Fairy? Did you ever believe that you would grow up, achieve your dreams, and live happily ever after? Did you ever find it inconceivable that pain and suffering would ever touch your life? As small children, we were all idealists. We viewed the world and our place in it through rose-colored glasses. We could not conceive it otherwise. This stage of our lives is referred to as the Age of Innocence. It is, however, short-lived. Inevitably, life will present us with conflicts that will bring about disillusions and suffering. We discover that people lie, love is often conditional, and that society does not always punish the guilty or protect the innocent. We all learn through trials (conflicts) that the world and its inhabitants are not perfect, and neither are we. Today we are going to look at a course followed by many of the characters in great literature and by each one of us as well. We will easily recognize the path and its markings because it is the same one we continue to travel. It leads us from the Age of Innocence and through conflict initiates us into the reality of life. In this structure, one grows only as a result of suffering and pain. Appropriately, it is called the Heroic Journey.

The Lesson

Input/Model/Check for Understanding/Practice:

Teach the four stages of the Heroic Journey:

Innocence: We are one with a perfect world. Suffering is minimal and short-lived. Death does not exist, and our lives are happy.

Initiation: We become aware of evil. We discover that the world is not fair; people, even those we love the most, will fail us; and we will all die.

Chaos: Through conflict (man vs. man, man vs. nature, man vs. himself) we struggle to make sense of the world. At this point, we come to terms with the discrepancies of our world and move forward into resolution, or deny that they exist and move back toward denial and into further chaos.

Resolution: Those who advance to this stage have resolved the conflict(s), used that information to make some sense of the world, and, in doing so, come to terms with one of life's realities.

Teach the three types of conflict:

All conflict, in life or in literature, falls into one of the following three categories:

1. Man Versus Man—Man is in conflict with another, or with society at large.

2. Man Versus Nature—Man in conflict with the forces of the natural world.

3. Man Versus Himself—Man in conflict with himself, as he struggles to make a decision, to come to terms with a physical, mental, emotional, or spiritual dilemma.

Read aloud one or more children's or young adult stories and discuss and chart with the class how the main character moves through the stage of the journey. Use examples from forms of nonprint text (films, television) as well.

Students read and discuss "Miracle on the Bayou." Teacher leads discussion toward identifying the four stages of the journey and the predominant conflict in the story, using textual evidence.

Innocence: Depiction of girls as they discover BooBoo's puppies and celebrate new life. ("Each arrival greeted with squeals of delight." "I want to keep the white one.")

Initiation: BooBoo and her puppies get sick. ("We took BooBoo and her seven pups . . . to Dr. Landon.")

Chaos: Narrator struggles to make sense of death. Man versus Nature ("It was, and remains to be, one of my saddest memories . . .")

Resolution: Another new life (Dandy) is brought into family, celebrated and also lost. (" . . . sisters and I watched with an understanding we could not yet comprehend . . .")

The Wrap-Up

Closure:

Students write an explanation of the heroic journey and use it as their ticket out of class.

Independent Practice:

Students read three selections (teacher or student choice) and plot the heroic journey in each, citing supporting textual evidence.

or

Students write a response to literature essay critiquing the author's use of the heroic journey framework.

Assessment:

Essay Scoring Guide (Key Resource 4.3 from Lesson 1)

Reteach:

If necessary.

Added Note:

The poem "After a While" is an excellent choice as a set or companion piece to this lesson. The short story "A Boy and His Dog" as well as the excerpt from *A Day No Pigs Would Die* are excellent examples of the journey motif.

KEY RESOURCE 4.5

Miracle on the Bayou

by Lorraine LaCroix

BooBoo had seven puppies that cold February in 1963. My Dad said she could have one litter—that it was somehow her right. She chose to have them in a dirt-packed hole under the house. My older sister and I sent LuLu (she was, after all, the smallest and we were still able to tell her what to do) under the house to retrieve the pups.

Polly and I waited silently in the manner of all expectant parents until LuLu returned with one pup and then another. Each new arrival was greeted with squeals of delight. "Isn't this one cute?" "I want to keep the white one." Or "Look how fat this one is." There were seven all together. My sisters and I had never been happier, and BooBoo and her puppies (we later discovered) had never been so sick.

We took BooBoo and her pups, wrapped in old towels warm from the dryer, to Dr. Landon. The diagnosis was pneumonia and the prognosis worse: We could save BooBoo only if she stopped nursing her pups. He would prescribe medication for them all, but if BooBoo were to survive, she would have to channel all her strength toward her own recovery. The puppies, he believed, had little chance of recovery without their mother's milk. But we could try.

Of course there was no question. We separated BooBoo from her puppies and set about the task of nursing them all back to health. We purchased a case of condensed milk from Winn Dixie, bought baby bottles from Boudreaux's Drugstore and set a schedule for feeding the puppies every two hours. Even with my sisters and I working together, it proved to be a daunting task: getting up several times a night, washing bottles and warming milk, watching as each pup grew weaker and weaker and—worst of all—the pitiful sound of scratching paws on the other side of the garage door.

In early spring Daddy buried seven puppies in a flower bed on a bluff overlooking Horseshoe Bayou. It was, and remains to be, one of my saddest memories: seven wooden crosses overlooking the Tchfuncte River.

BooBoo slowly regained her strength, but not her spirit. Once a dog full of energy, whose favorite pastimes were roughhousing with my sisters and I or running wild with the other neighborhood canines, she was now listless and uninterested. The harder we tried to bring her back, the further she withdrew. All our efforts proved pointless.

My father's habit was to walk on the bayou with BooBoo every evening. It was on one of these walks weeks later that the miracle occurred. BooBoo and Daddy became separated, and when he found her sometime later, she was not alone. In her mouth, caressed as softly as a pup, BooBoo carried a small brown wild rabbit. My Dad, who had been raised on the bayous and was very knowledgeable about local wildlife, knew that it was impossible to take a wild rabbit into captivity—and have it survive. They left the rabbit. However, the next evening on the same walk, BooBoo presented Daddy with another baby rabbit, dropping it at my father's feet and looking up as if to ask, "Can't I keep it?"

That night we placed the small rabbit (we named her Dandy because she loved dandelions) in the breezeway inside a large boot box filled with torn newspaper. When we awoke the next morning, we found that BooBoo had squeezed her way into the box, where she cradled Dandy next to her chest and between her front paws.

It was the beginning of what can only be described as an incredible relationship between two animals. BooBoo literally became Dandy's mother, watching over her, playing with her, even cleaning her as she would one of her own.

We entered Dandy in the Saint Tammany Parish Fair that October and won a blue ribbon. The following spring Daddy called a family meeting and explained to us that it was time for Dandy to return to the woods, that it was nature's way.

It was a ceremony of sorts, my father's way. BooBoo sat silently at Daddy's heels and Polly, LuLu, and I stood by and watched with an understanding we could not yet comprehend, as he lifted the latch from the cage and released Dandy to return to her home.

KEY RESOURCE 4.6

The Heroic Journey

Innocence:

Initiation:

Chaos (Man vs. Man, Man vs. Nature, or Man vs. Himself):

Resolution:

LESSON 3

Finding Themes in Literature Through Art

The Setup

Purpose:

To offer students an understanding and appreciation of how an author uses a storyline to develop universal themes within the text.

Objective:

Students will evaluate several selections of short fiction, determine theme(s), and support their choices with textual evidence; or students will read a fiction selection, determine the theme, and support their choice in an essay.

Materials Provided:

Story: "Boarding Flight 64" by Lorraine LaCroix
Handout: "Broad-Based Themes"
Worksheet: "Paired Themes in Short Fiction"
Essay Scoring Guide (Key Resource 4.3 from Lesson 1)

Materials to Be Collected:

Several pieces of short fiction that will provide rich examples of broad-based themes.
A collection of Norman Rockwell prints (or other art that does a good job of capturing life in print).

Optional Materials:

Stories from *Chicken Soup for the Teenage Soul*
A collection of photographs by Dorthea Lange or Len Bernstein.

Set:

Stories contain messages or lessons that lead the reader to reflect on the human dilemma. These themes may be major or minor, broad-based or specific, and developed through the characters' thoughts, words, or actions. A close examination of a text, one that goes beyond the question, "What is the author's message?" will often reflect myriad themes that add to our enjoyment of the text and provide a rich context from which we can begin our conversations about a literary work.

The Lesson

Input/Model/Check for Understanding/Practice:

Students read the short story "Boarding Flight 64" and are given a copy of the "Broad-Based Themes" handout.

Teacher asks students how several of these themes might apply to the work. Certainly a case could be made for Balance Versus Addiction (girls, as well as the mother, move out of addiction into balance) or Forgiveness Versus Resentment (one girl is able to forgive, the other cannot move out of resentment).

Teacher makes the connection between literature and art:

Art has its own language. Try to read the language of the painting or a photograph. How is looking at this art like reading? How does the author develop character? Create tension? Set mood? Begin by asking yourself what you see. This will help you to focus on the parts that lend themselves to the whole. How does the author's choice of colors contribute to the meaning of the piece? What do the lines in the art suggest? (Horizontal lines have a calming effect. Vertical lines suggest a rigid mood, and curvy lines tend to promote rhythm.) What do you feel or experience when you look at the work?

Teacher posts several pictures/photos (which depict a slice of life) on the walls of the classroom. Students move from picture to picture, using the "Broad-Based Themes" handout and "Paired Themes" worksheet to begin to generate ideas about the theme(s) they see in prints.

Whole class discussion follows.

Students read and discuss a short story (teacher's choice) in groups of three or four. Students decide which themes are present in the work and work together to find quotes that substantiate their claims. Additionally, students should come to a conclusion regarding their choice of the main theme of the work.

Whole class discussion follows.

The Wrap-Up

Closure:

Students partner-teach (paired students teach each other) their understanding of theme and the connection between literature and art in regard to this element.

Independent Practice:

Students work independently to complete an analysis of theme in a short story and to write a response to literature essay based on those findings.

Assessment:

Essay Scoring Guide (Key Resource 4.3 from Lesson 1)

Reteach:

If necessary.

KEY RESOURCE 4.7

Boarding Flight 64

by Lorraine LaCroix

"I want to sit in the seat by the window!" LuLu screamed as she ran down the ramp toward Gate 41B.

"We're going to share it, remember?" I reminded her as my feet struggled to keep up with her pace and still hold on to an armful of books, papers, pencils, cards, and other critical supplies I wanted to have with me on the plane.

LuLu skipped her way down the ramp, as if she were going to a picnic in the park. She had always been small for her age. She tanned naturally, and her hair was streaked with sunshine, in places almost white. Her face was more cute than pretty and her spirit, even as a child, soared above us all.

Polly, my older sister, walked silently, her legs taking long determined strides and her focus steadily forward, as if a glance to the side might throw her off course. Usually made up in heavy makeup and big hair, today she was more a shadow of herself. Her hair was combed back and she wore little or no artificial color. Although barely a woman herself, she was our rock, the constant who held my sisters and I together.

Mama walked with us, her head down—silent.

It had all happened so quickly. Polly running away, the phone call telling us that the police had found her, the trip to the courthouse to talk with the judge, the packing and finally the trip to the airport.

The loudspeaker announced: "Flight 64 to New Orleans, now boarding Gate 41B. All passengers are to report to the gate for loading." Our pace quickened, as Mama reached in her big purse to sort out the tickets and baggage claims from the boarding passes and located them just as we turned the corner to the gate. She handed each one of us our passes and the tickets and claims to the stewardess.

"They're traveling alone," she said, "their father is going to meet them in New Orleans."

The loud speaker broke in again: "Last call for passengers boarding Flight 64 to New Orleans. All passengers report to the boarding gate for immediate loading." Mama picked up LuLu first and gave her a big hug. She asked her if she had any money in case she ran out of candy, and LuLu, of course, took her up on her offer. (My sisters and I had learned to get what we could, when we could. You never knew if or when the tide would change with Mama.) LuLu took the dollar bills and refusing to take the stewardess' hand, waited instead on the side lines for Polly and I to say our goodbyes.

It was harder for me, because I remembered the old Mama, Mama before. The beautiful water ballerina who taught me how to swim, the funny lady who survived by finding humor—in even the most dire circumstances—who taught me how to laugh, and the artist who sat hour upon hour on our front porch painting with her oils who taught me how to create. But that had been a long time ago, and so much had happened since. I walked up to her now, threw my arms around her hips, and when she reached down, I looked up and kissed her cheek, surprised to find it wet with tears.

My sisters and I boarded the plane like age-old veterans. After all, none of this was new to us. We were used to the unexpected. To my sisters and I it had become the norm, a way of life. We took in stride the sudden moves from apartments to houses and back again. We had refined the practice of signing into new schools and searching out and making new friends. It no longer bothered us to rummage through an empty refrigerator, and come up with bologna sandwiches for dinner. Amazingly, we had even come to accept the endless trail of men in and out of our house, the midnight beatings and our beautiful drunk mother. We had no way of knowing that this trip, this turn of events would mark any real difference in our lives. Our excursion alone to New Orleans that morning in May meant relatively little to us. It was just something else, another knot, another hurdle to get over to survive another day.

Polly took LuLu by one hand, me by the other and headed down the ramp. She never even looked back.

Addendum:

My sisters and I grew up happy and secure with our father on the bayous of Louisiana. Twenty years later, when my mother contracted cancer, I returned to California to care for her. She, no longer able to drink, and I, wanting so much to reunite with her, found our way to each other. Over the next decade, and until her death in 1997, I was able to come to know and love one of the brightest, funniest, and kindest women I have ever known. It was then, and remains to be, one of life's greatest gifts to me. On April 20, 1997, my mother slipped into a coma and died of the cancer she had fought against for so many years. LuLu was there with me. We held her together as she passed away from us. Polly was not able to make the trip.

KEY RESOURCE 4.8

Broad-Based Themes

Adaptation Versus Alienation: Man naturally seeks a place among his peers. Alienation moves away from his natural state.

Balance Versus Addiction: The natural world seeks balance. Addiction produces chaos.

Change Versus Status Quo: Man naturally seeks to maintain the status quo. Change can be viewed as good or bad, but it is always inevitable.

Community Versus the Individual: Community members work together and the individual works alone. Communities share common values and the individual follows his own set of values.

Conflict Versus Cooperation: Cooperation is composed of like forces working in concert and is required for a group to advance. Conflict is composed of opposing forces. Conflict may involve natural or manmade forces and is either internal or external in nature. Conflict may be a precursor to change.

Dreams Versus Reality: In dreams we live out of our imagination. In day-to-day life we live out of our reality.

Fate Versus Free Will: All events are predetermined or all events are the results of conscious decisions men have made.

Forgiveness Versus Resentment: The decision to let go or to hold on.

Good Versus Evil: They may coexist. One may overcome the other.

Hope Versus Desperation: Cannot coexist.

Independence Versus Dependence: Both may be viewed as a negative or a positive force.

Love Versus Hate: Often separated by a thin line.

Order Versus Chaos: Chaos is sometimes necessary and may precede order.

Power Versus Powerlessness: Power is the ability to influence, may be used or abused, and either attracts or repels.

Success Versus Failure: Is often seen as the ultimate indicator of man's worth.

Survival Versus Extinction: Survival can be viewed as physical, mental, emotional, or spiritual. Extinction claims the weakest of its kind.

Youth Versus Maturity: The generation gap.

KEY RESOURCES 4.9

Paired Themes in Short Fiction

Story/Picture: _____ Theme: _____ Evidence: _____ _____ _____ _____ _____ _____ _____ _____	Story/Picture: _____ Theme: _____ Evidence: _____ _____ _____ _____ _____ _____ _____ _____
Story/Picture: _____ Theme: _____ Evidence: _____ _____ _____ _____ _____ _____ _____ _____	Story/Picture: _____ Theme: _____ Evidence: _____ _____ _____ _____ _____ _____ _____ _____

LESSON 4

The Important Questions

The Setup

Purpose:

To offer students an understanding and appreciation of how to pose questions to gain a deeper understanding of text.

Objective:

Students will evaluate several selections of fiction and write Level 1, 2, and 3 Questions pertaining to the text.

Materials Provided:

Story: "Blue Velvet" by Lorraine LaCroix

Materials to Be Collected:

Book of commonly read fairy tales
Several pieces of short fiction

Optional Materials:

Selections from *Reader's Digest*

Set:

There is an art to questioning. How a question is initially posed or what questions are asked as a follow-up to a response can make a substantial difference. Some children are naturally more inquisitive or talkative than others. For instance, one preschooler may return home full of stories about the day's events. Another may volunteer little, if any, information. This child, if asked how his day went, will usually respond in one word: "fine" or "OK." Occasionally, the child withholds information we would consider important. When the child is subsequently questioned about why he or she did not offer this information, the response may well be, "because you didn't ask me." The same is true of literature. If we are to come to a deeper, greater understanding of the text, we need to first learn how to pose questions that will lead us to other layers of meaning.

The Lesson

Input/Model/Check for Understanding/Practice:

There are three types of questions that can be used to drive conversation about text. They are referred to as Level 1, 2, and 3 Questions. Following is an explanation of each, using a familiar fairy tale, "Cinderella," as the model.

Level 1 Questions:

The answers to these questions can be found "on the line" directly in the text.

Examples: How many stepsisters did Cinderella have? What were some of Cinderella's jobs? What event were the stepsisters and Cinderella looking forward to?

Answers: The answers to these questions are found directly in the text. The reader is told explicitly that there are two stepsisters, that Cinderella swept the cinders, and that they were all looking forward to attending the ball.

Note: These questions often begin with the words Who? What? Where? When?

Level 2 Questions:

The answers to these questions can be found "in between the lines" and are easily inferred.

Examples: Why did Cinderella's stepmother not want her to go to the ball? How did this make Cinderella feel?

Answers: It is never directly stated in the tale, but one can logically draw the conclusions that the stepmother did not want Cinderella to attend the ball because she wanted her daughters to catch the prince's eye, and that Cinderella was very sad.

Note: These questions often begin with the words Why? or How?

Level 3 Questions:

The answers to these questions cannot be found in the text; they are "off the line." These questions contain no specific elements of the story itself and are often rhetorical in nature. They are, in large part, universal questions that concern the human dilemma. Level 3 questions force the reader to consider the text in a new light, will promote lively discussion, and often uncover the prevailing theme in the story.

Example: Can a mother truly love like her own a child who is not her own?

Answer: Of course, there is no one answer to this question, which speaks to the very core of this fairy tale and its universal nature.

Note: These questions are created without using any specifics attached to the text. There is never a mention of the main character, for example. The dilemma this character faces is the dilemma we all face together. Therefore, the main character becomes the universal "we."

Other models: Use other fairy tales. For instance, "Snow White and the Seven Dwarfs" may lead to a discussion about vanity and "The Three Little Pigs" to a discussion about responsibility.

Students are given a copy of "Blue Velvet" and work in pairs to read and then develop three Level 1 Questions, two Level 2 Questions, and one Level 3 Question.

Some of their questions may be the following:

Level 1: Who are the main characters in the story? (Lorrie and her dad) What was the name of the school the main character attended? (Covington Junior High) Why didn't she ask LeRoy to go to the prom with her? (Girls didn't ask boys to proms.)

Level 2: At the beginning of the story, how did Lorrie feel about the upcoming prom? (excited) How did she feel about the prom when it became clear that she was not going to be asked? (sad, left out)

Level 3: Can we make our dreams come true by living out of our imaginations, by creating a mental image of a dream realized in our minds?

The Wrap-up

Closure:

Students exchange the questions they wrote on "Blue Velvet," answer Level 1 and Level 2 Questions, and remark on the Level 3 Question.

Independent Practice:

Students read a text selected by the teacher and write Level 1, 2, and 3 Questions.

Assessment:

Questions are returned to teacher, who makes comments based on the quality of those questions.

Reteach:

If necessary.

KEY RESOURCE 4.10

Blue Velvet

By Lorraine LaCroix

It was my last year at Covington Junior High School, but I remember it as vividly as if it were yesterday. My girlfriends and I had talked of little else for weeks—the prom, what we were going to wear, who we wanted to go with, how the gym would be decorated, what songs they would play. There wasn't a stone, a detail of the evening, that we had left unturned. And, as the date grew nearer, the pieces began to fall into place. John Turner, the great looking guy who sat in front of me in World Geography, had asked Janice. Melinda was going with Steve Matson, and everyone knew Lucy would end up going with John McLaughlin.

I was the only one unaccounted for, the only one without a date. Even if someone had asked me (which, by the way, did not happen) I only had eyes for one boy—LeRoy Jacobs. He was smart, tall, dark, and handsome. And, he was somewhat shy and aloof, which gave him an added aura of mystery. I dreamed of walking onto the dance floor and being carried away in LeRoy's arms. I dreamed of sitting in Covington High's bleachers on chilly October nights, wearing his ring and watching him play football. And yes, I even dreamed of one day becoming Mrs. LeRoy Jacobs, and spent hours practicing writing my married name.

Although I shared my fantasies with my girlfriends, they knew—and in my heart of hearts so did I—that LeRoy would never ask me to the prom. There were, after all, lots of other prettier, more popular girls he could choose from. And yet, my friends and I never said anything. It was fun to pretend that we'd all be together that night.

As the date of the prom grew nearer, and more and more couples began to plan for the night (including LeRoy and his date—whose name now eludes me), my friends, sensing my sadness, talked less of the prom. (No one went to the prom alone. No date, no prom.) Although their intentions were good, they were somewhat misplaced. Their silence only served to deepen my pain, to once more engrave on my fragile spirit, that sense of being not quite good enough. I wanted now, more than any other time I could remember, to be a part of something—to go to the prom.

As the date of the prom grew closer, it became very clear that I was not going to be asked, by LeRoy or anyone else. Trained well in the southern way, I pretended it didn't matter and even joked about it. The tears I shed were silent. I didn't think anyone could hear, but as it turned out, I was wrong. I was very wrong.

A staunch patriot, Daddy never forgot to hang the American flag on national holidays—and the holidays that he declared. I awoke one morning to find the flag up and Daddy drinking coffee. He had declared a holiday, just for the two of us. By way of celebration, we would skip school and work and drive to New Orleans together.

It was a magical day. We had lunch in the French Quarter. He took me to a beauty salon and had my hair cut and curled in one of the latest fashion, a bob, and bought me a beautiful new dress (pink under white lace) at the Chubby Shop on Drier Street.

The trip across Lake Ponchatrain back to Covington took about an hour. We crossed a twenty-four-mile stretch of bridge over the lake, mile after mile of blue-grey water stretching as far as the eye could see. As we approached the piney woods of the north shore, my Dad popped the question: "Lorrie, would you allow me the pleasure of escorting you to your prom tomorrow night?" I was taken aback, shocked, and unprepared to answer. I felt stunned, surprised, appalled, and excited all at once. My mind raced ahead into the next night. Go to the dance with my Dad? What would everyone think? But they all knew Daddy. If I did have him as a "date," I could go to the prom and sit with my friends. I could see the gym lit with purple and pink paper lanterns, the tables decorated with light blue tablecloths and pastel candles. I could wear my new dress. I could see LeRoy, and I could hear all my favorite songs. I knew there might be a social price to pay, but I also knew, with absolute certainty, that it would be worth it. "Yes," I told him, "I will."

At 7:00 p.m. the following evening, I walked into the living room and Daddy was standing there, dressed in his suit and holding an orchid corsage, which he pinned on my new dress. Most girls only dream of being Cinderella. At that moment in time, the fairy tale came alive for me, and I was her, going to the ball with my Prince Charming.

Everything was just as I had envisioned it to be, and Daddy was great fun. He danced with my girlfriends and me and kept us all laughing. LeRoy was there, sitting with his date on the other side of the gym. Going to the prom with your Dad was one thing, asking a boy to dance with you was quite another. Needless to say, my Dad was my only dance partner.

But it was, after all, my enchanted evening. So, I really shouldn't question where my courage came from when the DJ announced that the last dance of the night would be lady's choice, and I was the first one out of my seat. I can remember every deliberate step I took across the floor to the other side of the gym where LeRoy was sitting with his date. I looked at him, and without as much as a hesitation asked, "LeRoy, will you dance with me?" He got out of his seat, escorted me to the center of the floor, put his arm around my waist, and in the shadow of paper lanterns and candlelight, we glided across the gym floor to Bobby Vinton's "Blue Velvet."

LESSON 5

In Search of Poetry—Found Poems

The Setup

Purpose:

To offer students an understanding and appreciation for the beauty of language. To offer students an understanding and appreciation for the art of summarizing, discriminating that text that goes to the very essence of the writing.

Objective:

Students will evaluate several selections of short nonfiction/fiction and "pull" phrases that represent the narrative or the essence of the message contained in the prose text, creating a poem.

Materials Provided:

Excerpt from Young Chief Joseph's Speech to Congress (1879)
Sample found poem drawn from the text.

Materials to Be Collected:

Several pieces of nonfiction/fiction that contains rich language.

Optional Materials:

Speech: Senator George Graham Vest's Eulogy on the Dog
Story: "Mother and Daughter" by Gary Soto (from the book *Baseball in April*)
Chapter 19 from John Steinbeck's *The Grapes of Wrath*

Set:

When we write about literature, our task is to maintain a careful balance between our paraphrase of the work and the author's own words. Often, the language, the exact words and phrases, and the order in which the author places them are so powerful that our choices become very difficult. Today we are going to look at a strategy that grants us license to use these dynamic words and phrases chosen by the author and to re-create the work in another genre, a poem. This new work then becomes a collaboration between the author and yourself.

The Lesson

Input/Mode/Check for Understanding/Practice:

Explain to students that their finished poem can be a narrative poem or an image poem. They should read a text through completely and decide which type of poem they are going to create before "finding" the first lines of the poem. This step is necessary because the decision will guide your choices, beginning with the first phrase.

Teacher and class read together the excerpt of Chief Joseph's Speech to Congress and decide that, because Joseph is using the story of the Nez Perces to drive his argument, it is appropriate that we choose to write a narrative poem based on the text.

Teacher uses the beginning excerpt of Chief Joseph's Speech to Congress as a model to teach the strategy. Reread with students the first paragraph of the speech. Explain to students that you now are going to go through the first paragraph again and highlight two to four phrases (*not sentences*) that you feel do the best job of telling the story. It is important to explain at this juncture that certainly a number of phrases would accomplish this end; you are simply sharing your choices.

Highlight the following, which will be lifted directly from the text:

show you my heart

white people to understand my people

Indian is like a wild animal. This is a great mistake

words to speak the truth.

Then, write your first lines of the poem, eliminating words when they are not necessary, capitalizing the first word in each line and adding punctuation:

Show you my heart

White people to understand my people

Indian a wild animal, great mistake

Words to speak the truth.

Note that the third phrase chosen from this paragraph (Indian is like a wild animal. This is a great mistake) was pared down again to become: Indian a wild animal, great mistake. A comma was inserted and each word that began a line of poetry was capitalized.

Direct students to the second paragraph, and repeat the same process.

Father was chief before me

No stain on his hands of the blood of a white man

Becomes:

Father chief before me

No stain on his hands of blood of white man

It is important to instruct students at this point that their task is to retain meaning with as few words as possible.

These two lines can then be added to the four lines pulled from the first paragraph or they may stand on their own and become the second stanza of the poem.

For best results, students should move forward, pulling text and forming lines of poetry and leave the demarcation of stanzas for their final editing.

Go through the next six paragraphs of the text and have students work in groups/pairs and then on their own to pull phrases for their individual poems.

When students move to editing their found poems, they make their own choices regarding:

Lines per stanza

What lines, if any, they want repeated (often placed at the beginning or end of each stanza)

Title (may or may not retain the title of the original work)

Their final step is to list the authors of the poem. In this chase, it would be Chief Joseph and (*name of the student*).

Added note: It is important to stress that the only words they may include in their poems are the exact words contained in the original text. At the editing stage, I allow for the addition of an article (a, the) where needed or an occasional change in verb tense to maintain the rhythm established in the poem.

Students practice strategy working with various selections. Students may work individually on a piece of text, come together and share with a group who has used the same text, and collaborate on a polished copy. Or they may work in pairs or individually to create these poems.

The Wrap-Up

Closure:

Students (groups/pairs/individuals) share their finished found poems with class. (Great opportunity to reinforce the elements of a good dramatic reading.)

Independent Practice:

Students write a found poem on their own.

Assessment:

Teacher reads poems and offers comments.

Reteach:

If necessary.

Added Note:

Optional materials serve as excellent examples of rich material and work well with this activity. It is also a great idea to pull from whatever novels you are (or will be) reading as a whole class. I have found that using this activity as a precursor to writing about literature goes a long way toward improving the rhetorical effectiveness of student essays.

KEY RESOURCE 4.11

Young Chief Joseph's Speech to Congress (1879)

My friends, I have been asked to show you my heart. I am glad to have a chance to do so. I want the white people to understand my people. Some of you think an Indian is like a wild animal. This is a great mistake. I will tell you all about our people, and then you can judge whether an Indian is a man or not. I believe much trouble and blood would be saved if we opened our hearts more. I will tell you in my way how the Indian sees things. The white man has more words to tell you how they look to him, but it does not require many words to speak the truth. What I have to say will come from my heart, and I will speak with a straight tongue. Ah-cum-kin-I-ma-me-hut (the Great Spirit) is looking at me, and will hear me.

My name is In-mut-too-yah-lat-lat (Thunder traveling over the Mountains). I am chief of the Wal-lam-wat-kin band of Chute-pe-lu, or Nez Perces (nose-pierced Indians). I was born in Eastern Oregon, thirty-eight winters ago. My father was chief before me. When a young man, he was called Joseph by Mr. Spaulding, a missionary. He died a few years ago. There was no stain on his hands of the blood of a white man. He left a good name on the earth. He advised me well for my people.

Our fathers gave us many laws, which they had learned from their fathers. These laws were good. They told us to treat all men as they treated us; that we should never be the first to break a bargain; that it was a disgrace to tell a lie; that we should speak only the truth; that it was a shame for one man to take from another his wife, or his property without paying for it. We were taught to believe that the Great Spirit sees and hears everything, and that he never forgets; that hereafter he will give every man a spirit-home according to his deserts; if he has been a good man, he will have a good home; if he has been a bad man, he will have a bad home. This I believe, and all my people believe the same.

We did not know there were other people besides the Indian until about one hundred winters ago, when some men with white faces came to our country. They brought many things with them to trade for furs and skins. They brought tobacco, which was new to us. They brought guns with flint stones on them, which frightened our women and children. Our people could not talk with these white-faced men, but they used signs which all people understand. These men were Frenchmen, and they called our people "Nez Perces," because they wore rings in their noses for ornaments. Although very few of our people wear them now, we are still called by the same name. These French trappers said a great many things to our fathers, which have been planted in our hearts. Some were good for us, but some were bad. Our people were divided in opinion about these men. Some thought they taught more bad than good. An Indian respects a brave man, but he despises a coward. He loves a straight tongue, but he hates a forked tongue. The French trappers told us some truths and some lies.

The first white men of your people who came to our country were named Lewis and Clarke. They also brought many things that our people had never seen. They talked straight, and our people gave them a great feast, as a proof that their hearts were friendly. These men were very kind. They made presents to our chiefs and our people made presents to them. We had a great many horses, of which we gave them what they needed, and they gave us guns and tobacco in return. All the Nez Perces made friends with Lewis and Clarke, and agreed to let them pass through their country, and never to make a war on white men. This promise the Nez Perces have never broken. No white man can accuse them of bad faith, and speak with a straight tongue. It has always been the pride of the Nez Perces that they were the friends of the white men. When my father was a young man there came to our country a white man (Rev. Mr. Spaulding) who talked spirit law. He won the affections of our people because he spoke good things to them. At first he did not say anything about white men wanting to settle on our lands. Nothing was said about that until about twenty winters ago, when a number of white people came into our country and built houses and made farms. At first our people made no complaint. They thought there was room enough for all to live in peace, and they were learning many things from the white men that seemed good. But we soon found that the white men were growing rich very fast, and were greedy to possess everything the Indian had. My father was the first to see through the schemes of the white men, and he warned his tribe to be careful about trading with them. He had suspicion of men who seemed so anxious to make money. I was a boy then, but I remember well my father's caution. He had sharper eyes than the rest of our people.

Next there came a white officer (Governor Stevens), who invited all the Nez Perces to a treaty council. After the council was opened he made known his heart. He said there was a great many white people in the country and many more would come; that he wanted the land marked out so that the Indians and white men could be separated. If they were to live in peace it was necessary, he said, that the Indians should have a country set apart for them, and in that country they must stay. My father, who represented his band, refused to have anything to do with the council, because he wished to be a free man. He claimed that no man owned any part of the earth, and a man could not sell what he did not own.

Mr. Spaulding took hold of my father's arm and said, "Come and sign the treaty." My father pushed him away, and said: "Why do you ask me to sign away my country? It is your business to talk to us about spirit matters, not to talk to us about parting with our land." Governor Stevens urged my father to sign the treaty, but he refused. "I will not sign your paper," he said; "you go where you please, so do I; you are not a child, I am no child; I can think for myself. No man can think for me. I have no other home than this. I will not give it up to any man. My people would have no home. Take away your paper. I will not touch it with my hand."

KEY RESOURCE 4.12

Sample Found Poem

Chief Joseph Speaks to Congress

Show you my heart

White people to understand my people

Indian a wild animal, great mistake

Words to speak the truth.

Father chief before me

No stain on his hands of blood of white man.

Great Spirit sees and hears everything

Every man a spirit-home according to deserts

This I believe.

French trappers said a great many things

Taught more bad than good

Indian loves a straight tongue, hates a forked tongue.

Lewis & Clarke talked straight, made friends

Promises by Nez Perces never broken

White men growing rich fast, greedy to possess everything.

Land marked

Indians and white men separated

Father refused, wished to be free man.

Spaulding: "Come and sign treaty."

Father pushed away

Take away paper, I will not touch.

Written by Chief Joseph and edited by Lorraine LaCroix

Other Options:

Combine lines into one stanza.

Repeat the line "This I believe" or "Words to speak the truth" at the beginning or end of each stanza.

And there could be many more . . .

LESSON 6

"Poetry Is . . ."—An Introduction

The Setup

Purpose:

To offer students an overview of the many facets and interpretations of poetry as a genre.

Objective:

Students will clarify and define their personal definition of poetry and practice the elements of a good dramatic reading.

Materials Provided:

Handout: "Poetry Is . . ."
Handout: "Dramatic Reading Rubric" (Key Resource 3.2)

Materials to Be Made:

Poster of the Dramatic Reading Rubric

Set:

Teacher asks: "What is poetry?" Students journal in their notebooks. Class discussion follows:
Teacher asks: "Is it possible that you all have the correct answer?"
Teacher explains: "Yes, because there can be as many definitions as there are readers."
Teacher adds: "Can there be wrong answers to this question? Yes."
(Reaffirms that there may be multiple correct answers, but that there are certainly wrong answers as well. The only criteria is that their answer be supported by valid evidence or examples.)

The Lesson

Input:

Teacher says: "Lets consider how others have defined this type of writing." Teacher passes out the handout "Poetry Is . . ." Students read definitions silently.

Model:

Students are directed to a poster containing the Dramatic Reading Rubric and asked to look for the elements as the teacher reads.

Further Input:

Students are asked to use the highlighter or place check marks to designate their three favorite definitions of poetry and to mark them 1, 2, and 3. The teacher should explain that there are no wrong answers in this case; students may choose the definitions simply because they like the sounds of the words or it coincides with their understanding.

Check for Understanding:

Teacher works the room as they read, keeping students on task, and offering support.

Guided Practice/Check for Understanding:

Teacher calls on students at random to read their Number 1 definition. The student stands at his or her desk and reads, making an attempt to incorporate the elements of the Dramatic Reading Rubric. Teacher should be gentle but firm, offering praise and suggestions for improvement, then modeling what that element should "look like" when they are reading the definition. Follow same process for definition numbers 2 and 3. (Any number of active participation methods will work well for this exercise.)

The Wrap-Up

Closure:

Return to your journals and write two new definitions of poetry.

Independent Practice:

Students will choose a definition of poetry from the list (or create their own) and write a paragraph explaining and supporting their definition. Paragraphs are shared with class.

Assessment:

Memorize two definitions of poetry for Thursday quiz.

Reteach:

If necessary.

Notebook Requirement:

The handout of poetry definitions and the students' paragraphs supporting their choice become pages in their poetry notebook.

KEY RESOURCE 4.13

Poetry Is . . .

☞ . . . An expression of power and sensitivity in written form.
Author Unknown

☞ . . . A reflection of the world of yesterday and today.
Author Unknown

☞ . . . Something that lives like fire inside you.
F. Scott Fitzgerald

☞ . . . An experience with the color, flavor and magnificence of words.
Author Unknown

☞ . . . The heaven of the working reason.
Jacques Maritain

☞ . . . A comprehension of thought and feeling.
Author Unknown

☞ . . . A sword of lightning, ever unsheathed, which consumes the scabbard that would contain it.
Percy Bysshe Shelley

☞ . . . The universal language that the heart holds with nature and itself.
William Hazlitt

☞ . . . An adventure with figurative speech.
Author Unknown

☞ . . . A constellation of forms from serious and dramatic to lighthearted and nonsensical.
Author Unknown

☞ . . . An expression in rhyme, free verse or prose.
Author Unknown

☞ . . . The most direct and simple means of expressing oneself in words.
Northrop Frye

☞ . . . A challenging lesson in vocabulary, word choice and grammar.
Author Unknown

☞ . . . A distilled language response to life, to an event, to a moment.
Author Unknown

☞ . . . The rhythmical creation of beauty.
Edgar Allan Poe

☞ . . . A song intended to be read aloud, heard and savored.
Author Unknown

☞ . . . Freedom to exercise poetic license and take liberties not allowed in ordinary writing.
Author Unknown

☞ . . . As modern as the stuff of today and as old as the hills.
Author Unknown

LESSON 7

The Power of Words—Interpreting Poetry

The Setup

Purpose:

To offer students an appreciation for the power of words, especially those contained in the rhythms and sounds of poetry.

Objective:

Students will journal multiple interpretations of poetry, offer dramatic readings of same, and write a stanza of poetry in the style of Henry Wadsworth Longfellow.

Materials Provided:

Worksheet: "Changing Impressions"
Handout: "Dramatic Reading Rubric" (Key Resource 3.2)
Poems: "The Day Is Done" and "The Psalm of Life," both by Henry Wadsworth Longfellow

Optional Materials:

Poems: "Poetry Should Ride the Bus" by Ruth Forman, "Feelings About Words" by Mary O'Neill, and "Proud Words" by Carl Sandburg

Set:

Teacher asks: "Have you ever said something you didn't mean, and then wanted to take it back? Has anyone ever said something hurtful to you, and you wished the words would go away, but you know they cannot? Has anyone ever given you a compliment or praised your hard work, and those words stay and become part of who you are?"

At this point, I relate a personal story about an incident that occurred to me in the sixth grade. Teachers may, of course, want to draw from their own experience. The story goes like this: I was in the sixth grade, sitting in my classroom, working on a math problem. My teacher, Mrs. Sellers, was walking up and down the aisles checking our work. She stopped at my desk, put her hand on my back, leaned down, and said: "Lorrie, did anyone ever tell you what a smart little girl you are?" The truth of the matter is, no one ever had told me that. It may well be a coincidence, but if you check my report cards prior to the sixth grade, you'll find that my grades were average and, at least from my teachers' points of view, I had no special talents. There was not anything special about Lorrie LaCroix. After Mrs. Sellers and the sixth grade, I miraculously became an "A" student. I have to wonder, if that one moment in time had not occurred, how my life might have been different. Today, especially when I feel defeated and not too sure of myself, if I try, I can still feel Mrs. Sellers' hand on my back and hear her words again. I'm sure that Mrs. Sellers had no idea of the impact she was to have on me; she was simply being a "good teacher," encouraging her student to do her best.

Teacher adds: "It has been said that the word is mightier than the sword. And I would agree; words shape our feelings about who we are and how we fit into the world in which we live."

The Lesson

Input/Model:

Students are given copies of the "Changing Impressions" worksheet and the poem "The Day Is Done." They read the poem silently. After reading, students journal their first impressions of the poem (1- to 2-minute quick write on worksheet). Teacher reads the poem aloud. Students journal added impressions and understandings of the poem (1- to 2-minute quick write on worksheet). Teacher asks a student to read the poem aloud. Students journal again. Students share their impressions in small groups. Students journal added understanding of the poem based on that discussion. Class now discusses how multiple readings of a poem add to the understanding and appreciation of the work. Possible reasons: We simply hear more during subsequent readings of a poem; meaning can change significantly as it is presented through different voices, personalities, or perspectives; and discussions with others can add greatly to our interpretations.

Teacher reviews elements of an effective dramatic reading.

Guided Practice/Check for Understanding:

Students are given copies of the Dramatic Reading Rubric. They work in groups of three or four, reading the poem one stanza at a time in a round-robin fashion. Students critique presentations of others in the group using the Dramatic Reading Rubric.

Independent Practice:

Students are called on randomly to read aloud a portion of the poem (one or more stanzas).

Input:

Teacher calls attention to the poem's rhyme scheme (first stanza ABAB and other stanzas ABCB).

Model:

Teacher models how you can add additional lines to this poem by maintaining the same subject and rhyme pattern.

Example:

Read as I begin to *slumber*	A
Passing into the darkness that is *night*	B
That my dreams may be filled with *wonder*	A
And I will not awake in *fright.*	B

Guided Practice/Check for Understanding:

Teacher walks the room. Students work with a partner to create one or more new stanzas for the poem. Stanzas are shared, recorded, and posted as a new poem, created by the class.

The Wrap-Up

Independent Practice:

Students are given copies of the poem "The Psalm of Life" another "Changing Impressions" worksheet, and asked to read silently. The assignment will then be to record their first impressions of the work on their worksheets after a silent reading, a reading aloud, and at the conclusion of a conversation about the work (share poem with a family member or friend). Additionally, they should practice reading the poem aloud, referring back to their Dramatic Reading Rubric. After impressions are recorded, students write and add their own stanza to the poem, using the pattern established in the original work.

(New stanzas for the poem can be shared and posted in the classroom, displaying a second poem authored by the class.)

Closure:

Students prepare to leave the room, leaving out their "Psalm of Life" poem. Teacher calls on selected students to give a dramatic reading of one stanza. After each student reads, his or her row is dismissed.

Assessment:

Completion of journal entries and newly created stanza to be added to "Psalm of Life."

Reteach:

If necessary.

Notebook Requirement:

The two poems addressed in this lesson, as well as the new poem(s) created by the class, should be added to their poetry notebook.

KEY RESOURCE 4.14

Changing Impressions

Name _____

Date _____

Title of Poem _____

Author _____

Impressions after first silent reading: _____

_____

_____

_____

_____

Impressions after first oral reading: _____

_____

_____

_____

_____

Impressions after second oral reading: _____

_____

_____

_____

_____

Impressions after discussion of the reading: _____

_____

_____

_____

_____

KEY RESOURCE 4.15

The Day Is Done

by Henry Wadsworth Longfellow

The day is done, and the darkness
Falls from the wings of Night,—
As a feather is wafted downward
From an eagle in his flight.

I see the lights of the village
Gleam through the rain and the mist,
And a feeling of sadness comes o'er me
That my soul cannot resist:

A feeling of sadness and longing,
That is not akin to pain,
And resembles sorrow only
As the mist resembles the rain.

Come, read to me some poem,
Some simple and heartfelt lay,
That shall soothe this restless feeling,
And banish the thoughts of day.

Not from the grand old masters,
Not from the bards sublime,
Whose distant footsteps echo
Through the corridors of Time.

For, like strains of martial music,

Their mighty thoughts suggest

Life's endless toil and endeavor;

And to-night I long for rest.

Read from some humbler poet,

Whose songs gushed from his heart,

As showers from the clouds of summer,

Or tears from the eyelids start;

Who, through long days of labor,

And nights devoid of ease,

Still heard in his soul the music

Of wonderful melodies.

Such songs have power to quiet

The restless pulse of care,

And come like the benediction

That follows after prayer.

Then read from the treasured volume

The poem of thy choice,

And lend to the rhyme of the poet

The beauty of thy voice.

And the night shall be filled with music,

And the cares, that infest the day,

Shall fold their tents, like the Arabs,

And as silently steal away.

KEY RESOURCE 4.16

The Psalm of Life

by Henry Wadsworth Longfellow

Tell me not, in mournful numbers,

Life is but an empty dream!

For the soul is dead that slumbers,

And things are not what they seem.

Life is real! Life is earnest!

And the grave is not its goal;

Dust thou art, to dust returnest,

Was not spoken of the soul.

Not enjoyment, and not sorrow,

Is our destined end or way;

But to act, that each tomorrow

Find us farther than today.

Art is long, and Time is fleeting,

And our hearts, though stout and brave,

Still, like muffled drums, are beating

Funeral marches to the grave.

In the world's broad field of battle,

In the bivouac of Life,

Be not dumb, driven cattle!

Be a hero in the strife!

Trust no Future, howe'er pleasant!

Let the dead Past bury its dead!

Act, act in the living Present!

Heart within, and God o'erhead!

Lives of great men all remind us

We can make our lives sublime,

And, departing, leave behind us

Footprints on the sands of time;

Footprints, that perhaps another,

Sailing o'er life's solemn main,

A forlorn and shipwrecked brother,

Seeing, shall take heart again.

Let us, then, be up and doing,

With a heart for any fate;

Still achieving, still pursuing,

Learn to labor and to wait.

LESSON 8

"I'm Nobody! Who are you?"—
The Poetry of Emily Dickinson

The Setup

Purpose:

To offer students an understanding of the relationship among poets, their works, and their styles, and how these relationships play a part when interpreting poetry.

Objective:

Students will study the life and poetry of Emily Dickinson and consider the ways in which the poem reflects the poet.

Materials Provided:

Teacher Notes: Summation of Emily Dickinson's Life
Poems: "Because I could not stop for Death;" "I'm Nobody! Who are you?"; "'Nature' is what we see;" "If I should die;" "Apparently with no surprise;" "If I can stop one Heart from breaking;" and "Nature, the gentlest mother."

Materials to Be Collected:

Biographical reading material on Emily Dickinson, to be used by teacher when delivering input.

Set:

Teacher reads aloud, "Nature is what we see." Teacher then says, "Who do you imagine the author of this poem to be? Is it a man or is it a woman? Does the poet live in the city or in the country? How does the poet feel about nature? Why?" And so on. (Answers should bring the class to the consensus that it is a woman who lives in the country and who is consumed with a wonder of the natural world.) Explain that these suppositions are true. Conclude further that we can tell a great deal about a poet from the poetry he or she writes and vice versa; we can interpret and know a great deal more about a poem if we know the poet behind the words. Begin a discussion about Emily Dickinson and consider how her life is reflected in her poems.

The Lesson

**Input/Model:*

Teacher tells (or reads from biographical source) a story about Emily Dickinson. Students are asked *not* to write notes in their notebooks until the teacher has stopped reading. When the teacher stops after the first chunk of reading/information, they model note-taking by writing those details (notes) drawn from the reading that they consider to be the most significant.

Practice/Check for Understanding:

After the second and third chunks of reading, storytelling, and input, the teacher has students work with a partner to record notes as the teacher walks around the room checking for understanding.

Independent Practice:

Students listen and record notes on their own after the remaining reading chunks are given.

(*This strategy is called "attentive lecture." It encourages active listening and allows the teacher to model good note-taking skills.)

Input/Model:

Teacher passes out "Because I could not stop for Death—." The teacher asks, "What qualities do we find in this poem that would lead us to believe that it was one written by Emily Dickinson?" Answers: short length (two stanzas); lacks rhyme; use of the dash; subject is death and immortality; no title; important words are capitalized, regardless of their position in the poem.

Teacher then asks: "What is the meaning or the theme of this poem?" Students will most likely answer that it is a poem about death. Teacher explains that to understand the theme, the reader must know the meaning of every word. Teacher defines from a dictionary the words "immortality" (living after death), "haste" (hurry), and "civility" (politeness). Teacher leads students step by step to an interpretation: There is never a time that you are ready for death (I could not stop), but it will come (stopped for me), and it will come gently (kindly). The carriage (death) slowly drives (takes) one to another world where there is no work or joy (labor and leisure), but where the soul still survives (immortality). One might conclude that this is a poem in which the author acknowledges the inevitability of death, or at least the passage into another dimension.

Guided Practice:

Each student is given several poems written by the author. These poems are read aloud by the teacher and students. Students are then grouped or paired and asked to take two of these poems through the same process. Teacher asks: "What qualities do we find in the poem that distinguish it as being a poem written by Emily Dickinson?" (Consider the notes taken earlier in class.) Teacher asks: "What is the meaning or the theme of the poem?" (Students use dictionaries to define unfamiliar words.)

The Wrap-Up

Closure:

Students who have chosen the same poem come before the class and discuss the poem as a panel. Repeat for as many poems as time allows.

Independent Practice:

Students are asked to research other biographical works and poems by Emily Dickinson, to add at least three interesting facts to their short biography and two additional poems (with a brief interpretation of each) to their collection of works by the poet.

Assessment:

Completion of notes (in class) with the additional three facts and two poems chosen by the student, along with interpretations of them. Thursday quiz as well

Reteach:

If necessary.

Notebook Requirement:

Poems, interpretations, and biographical material about the author are to be included.

Additional Resources:

Videos or DVDs on the poet's life; readings of her poetry.

Added Note:

The included cursory "Summation of Emily Dickinson's Life" is intended as a resource for the teacher, but it certainly may be used as a student handout.

KEY RESOURCE 4.17

The Poems of Emily Dickinson

Because I could not stop for Death

Because I could not stop for Death—

He kindly stopped for me—

The Carriage held but just Ourselves—

And Immortality.

We slowly drove—He knew no haste

And I had put away

My labor and my leisure too,

For His Civility—

I'm Nobody! Who are you?

I'm Nobody! Who are you?

Are you—Nobody—too?

Then there's a pair of us!

Don't tell! they'd banish us—you know!

How dreary—to be—Somebody!

How public—like a Frog—

To tell your name—the livelong June—

To an admiring Bog

"Nature" is what we see—

"Nature" is what we see—

The Hill—the Afternoon—

Squirrel—Eclipse—the Bumble bee—

Nay—Nature is Heaven—

Nature is what we hear—

The Bobolink—the Sea—

Thunder—the Cricket—

Nay—Nature is Harmony—

Nature is what we know—

Yet have no art to say—

So impotent our Wisdom is

To her Simplicity

If I should die

If I should die,

And you should live—

And time should gurgle on—

Tis sweet to know that stocks will stand

When we with Daisies lie

Apparently with no surprise

Apparently with no surprise

To any happy Flower

The Frost beheads it at its play—

In accidental power—

The blond assassin passes on—

The Sun proceeds unmoved

To measure off another Day

For an Approving God.

If I can stop one Heart from breaking

If I can stop one Heart from breaking

I shall not live in vain

If I can ease one Life the Aching

Or cool one Pain

Or help one fainting Robin

Unto his Nest again

I shall not live in Vain.

Nature, the gentlest mother

Nature, the gentlest mother,

Impatient of no child,

The feeblest or the waywardest,

Her admonition mild

In forest and the hill

By traveler is heard,

Restraining rampant squirrel

Or too impetuous bird.

How fair her conversation.

A summer afternoon,—

Her household, her assembly;

And when the sun goes down

Her voice among the aisles

Incites the timid prayer

Of the minutest cricket.

The most unworthy flower.

When all the children sleep

She turns as long away

As will suffice to light her lamps;

Then, bending from the sky

With infinite affection

And infinite care,

Her golden finger on her lip,

Wills silence everywhere.

KEY RESOURCE 4.18

Summation of Emily Dickinson's Life

- Emily Dickinson 1830–1886

- One of America's finest poets

- Work unknown during her life; became famous posthumously

- Lived entire life in Amherst, Massachusetts

- Older brother Austin and younger sister Lavinia

- Strong attachment to her father

- May have been in love with Reverend Charles Wadsworth

- Became an eccentric recluse later in life; seldom left her room, appeared only occasionally, and always dressed in white

- Poems were not titled and often scribbled on little pieces of paper and stuffed in drawers or under her mattress

- Six poems published during her lifetime

- Others published after her death

- Poems were not titled (first line is commonly used as the title)

- Most poems short and unrhymed (free verse)

- Unconventional writer: first to use a dash (—) in her poems, capitalized and punctuated verse only as it pleased her, and made up a word if she could not find one that suited her purpose

- Famous topics: death and immortality, love, and nature

LESSON 9

A Self-Portrait—The Bio Poem

The Setup

Purpose:

To offer students an understanding and appreciation for poetry that is vividly descriptive and personally specific.

Objective:

Students will write an autobiographical poem.

Materials Provided:

"Bio Poem Formula and Example"
"Matt's Bio Poem"
"Bio Poem Worksheet"
"Character Traits" Handout
Bio Poem Rubric

Materials to Be Collected:

Class set of thesauruses.

Set:

Teacher says: "How many of you like to write poetry? How many of you don't like to write poetry? How many of you find poetry writing difficult? How many of you find poetry writing fun? We obviously have a mixed group. For those of you who struggle with writing poetry, today I am going to give you a fail-safe recipe for writing a poem and assign you a topic on which you are the absolute expert: yourself. It is called a Bio Poem, and it will be our first writing assignment of the unit.

The Lesson

Input/Model:

Teacher passes out "Bio Poem Formula and Example." Teacher explains each line in the Bio Poem formula and the corresponding example.

Added points the teacher should make:

Line 1: First name.

Line 2: Four words of description. These are four single words that describe the inner you. Students cannot use any unflattering or negative words to describe themselves. Refer them to the "Character Traits" handout if they are having difficulty finding the right words to describe themselves.

Line 3: A relative of . . . (person, place, or thing). This line should be completed with a phrase(s), not single words. For instance, a relative of the Thompson and Jones families would not be acceptable. Ask students to consider their grandparents and ancestors. From what countries did they immigrate? How did they make their living? They take this information and stretch it out. For instance, instead of Ireland the student could write "dreamers from the Emerald Isle"; instead of Mexico, the student could write "the ancient and proud Aztec warriors."

Lines 4 through 8: Each of these lines begin with the words written on the formula. For instance, students cannot write, "Afraid of . . ." They must begin that line with the words "Who fears . . ." The student will need additional lines to complete this portion of the poem. Who feels, Who needs, and so on are words that appear only once in the poem. For instance, after "Who feels" the students write the three things they fear, separating the ideas with commas or semicolons.

Lines 4 through 8 again: When students are completing these lines, it is imperative that they take single words or ideas and pull them out into a phrase using adjectives. They also must be as specific as possible. Students tend to be very general at this stage. Explain to them that the most interesting bio poems are poems that are specific and detailed. For instance, a student can write "Who would like his little sister to disappear" or "Who would like his little runt of a six-year-old sister—Darcy—to get lost permanently."

More on Lines 4 through 8: Students should be directed to address a topic no more than once anywhere in the poem. For instance, the student cannot write, "Who fears not being selected for the Los Altos Little League All-Star game . . ." and then write "Who would like to be a starting pitcher for the Anaheim Angels . . ."

Line 9: A resident of . . . Instruct students to let their imaginations soar here.

Line 10: Last name.

Added note: Throughout the poem students should attempt to mix the serious with the light and, again, to be specific and to personalize, personalize, personalize.

Additional Model:

Matt's Bio Poem.

Input:

Teacher passes out and discusses "Bio Poem Rubric."

Guided Practice/Checking for Understanding:

Teacher passes out the "Bio Poem Worksheet." Students work in pairs to write Line 2, four words of description, and Line 4, Lover of . . . Teacher walks room, checking for understanding.

Independent Practice/Checking for Understanding:

Students, using the "Bio Poem Formula," "Character Traits" handout, thesauruses, and "Bio Poem Rubric," work in groups or alone to complete a rough draft of their Bio Poem. Teacher must initial before students can begin polished copy.

The Wrap-Up

Closure:

Students share completed parts of their poem with class.

Independent Practice:

Writing the polished Bio Poem.

Assessment:

According to "Bio Poem Rubric."

Reteach:

If necessary.

Notebook Requirement:

Students' polished Bio Poems should be included in their poetry notebook. Students often add a visual of some sort, a picture of themselves, a self-portrait, or a creative border.

Added Note:

Students are told that the Bio Poems can be dated and framed and given as a gift. In this case, the Bio Poem becomes a snapshot of their inner selves at the age of twelve, thirteen, or fourteen. Poems framed with a picture make excellent presents for family members.

KEY RESOURCE 4.19

Bio Poem Formula and Example

Formula

Line 1	First name
Line 2	Four words of description
Line 3	A relative of (person, thing, or idea)
Line 4	Lover of (three ideas)
Line 5	Who feels (three ideas)
Line 6	Who needs (three ideas)
Line 7	Who fears (three ideas)
Line 8	Who would like (three ideas)
Line 9	A resident of (a real or imaginary place)
Line 10	Last name

Example

Kristin

Persistent, confident, independent, and daring

A relative of the movers and shakers of the hippie generation

Lover of the orange-gold sun just as it disappears over the horizon;

round soft black lab puppies (that her mom won't let her have until they move to a house) and

the color purple—on any and everything

Who feels she never has anything to wear (and her closet is too small);

you can never carry too many things in your purse—you should be prepared for anything; and

that Brian Daniels is the cutest boy in the seventh grade

Who needs to find the perfect thing to say and the perfect time to say it;

to do her homework every night (instead of talking to her friends Doretha and Margo); and

to be a little kinder to her little sister Mary

Who fears people obsessed with reality TV;

the knots on her rope of life; and

that feeling of loneliness, especially in a crowded room

Who would like to see life's mistakes come with erasers;

people liked for who they are, not what they are; and

to have one more precious day with her grandpa

A resident of a little blue house on the seashore, where the sun always shines and she lives happily ever after—forever.

Kelley

KEY RESOURCE 4.20

Matt's Bio Poem

About a Boy

Matt

Loyal, independent, respectful, competitive.

A relative of the old Scot-Irish clans of the Emerald Isles.

Lover of a little black cat with white paws named Boots Vondelle (we got her at Vons grocery);

the metallic sounds of Creed, Blink 182, and Ozzie Osbourne; and

his mom's smile.

Who feels student council elections should have more to do with a person's worth and less to do with a

person's appearance;

irritated when his parents say one thing and do another; and

a bike isn't worth having if it isn't a silver Beach Cruiser.

Who needs a job three hours a day throwing papers (to buy an electric guitar);

lifelong passes to Disneyland, California Adventure, and Raging Waters; and

to be a better friend to Nick.

Who fears not making the honor roll (especially when his dad finds out);

WWE (and The Rock and Mark Henry) being taken off TV; and

death itself.

Who would like Taylor (the girl with the soft brown eyes) to move back across the street;

five minutes with Babe Ruth; and

his little brother Nico to be banished from the face of the Earth.

Resident of a gray castle on a green hill, far, far away.

Bernard

KEY RESOURCE 4.21

Bio Poem Worksheet

Name _____   Date _____

[First name] _____

Four words of description _____   _____

_____   _____

A relative of _____

_____

_____

Lover of _____

_____

_____

Who feels _____

_____

_____

Who needs _____

_____

_____

Who fears _____

_____

_____

Who would like _____

_____

_____

A resident of _____

_____

[Last name] _____

KEY RESOURCE 4.22

Character Traits

adventurous
athletic

brave
bright

caring
charming
cheerful
committed
competitive
confident
contented
creative

daring
decisive
direct
disciplined

enthusiastic
even-tempered
expressive

fashionable
focused
free-spirited
friendly
funny

gregarious

high-spirited

independent
insightful
intelligent

kind

logical
loving
loyal

observant
optimistic
outgoing
outspoken

perceptive
persistent
persuasive
principled

respectful

self-reliant
sociable
stimulating
strong

tactful
talented
tenacious

unconventional

KEY RESOURCE 4.23

Bio Poem Rubric (Six Point)

To score a 6, your writing will

_____ be complete, grammatically correct, and contain phrases in lines 3 through 9

_____ have a creative title that engages the reader immediately

_____ vividly re-create the subject

_____ describe fully and offer examples of personal associations/tastes

_____ use sensory details, specific actions, and/or dialogue to help the reader visualize the subject

_____ use a variety of rhetorical structures and language to convey purpose, direction, and movement

_____ be fresh, creative, and original

To score a 5, your writing will

_____ be complete, grammatically correct, and contain phrases in lines 3 through 9

_____ have an creative title

_____ clearly define or identify the subject

_____ describe and offer examples of personal associations and tastes

_____ include enough detail to re-create the subject

_____ use some rhetorical devices

_____ be interesting and enthusiastic

To score a 4, your writing will

_____ be complete, grammatically correct, and contain some phrases in lines 3 through 9

_____ have an interesting title

_____ clearly define or identify the subject

_____ describe some personal associations and tastes

_____ use some details to begin to create an impression about the subject

_____ use too much or too little information

_____ be predictable, but still strong

To score a 3, your writing will

_____ be complete, contain few grammatical errors, and some phrases in lines 3 through 9

_____ have a general title that states subject's name or Bio Poem

_____ identify the subject

_____ state personal associations and taste

_____ contain few details, often organized as a listing

_____ offer too much information about the subject or leave out important information

_____ be predictable and shallow

To score a 2, your writing will

_____ not be fully complete and contain several grammatical errors

_____ may or may not contain a title

_____ state the subject

_____ reveal minimal personal associations and tastes

_____ contain only general, scanty information, often organized as a listing

To score a 1, your writing will

_____ not be complete

_____ have little or no information about the subject

LESSON 10

"All the world's a stage . . ."—Shakespeare and Figurative Language

The Setup

Purpose:

To offer students an understanding and appreciation for figurative language.

Objective:

Students will study the application of figurative language, specifically similes, metaphors, and personification, in three works by William Shakespeare.

Materials Provided:

Worksheet: "Similes, Metaphors, and Personification"
Poems: "The Seven Ages of Man," "He Jests at Scars," and "Like as the Waves" by William Shakespeare
"A Split Tree Still Grows," Anonymous
"Essay Scoring Guide" (Key Resource 4.3 from Lesson 1)

Materials to be collected:

Literature books. Most class anthologies will contain many examples of figurative language.

Optional materials:

Poems: "Barter" by Sara Teasdale, "Giraffes" by Sy Kahn, "March" by S. P. Russell, "The Pheasant" by R. Tristram Coffin, and "Steam Shovel" by Charles Malam.

Set:

Teacher writes following couplets on the board and asks students to consider which line creates a sharper image.

A. The log house was on the side of the mountain.

The log house clung fiercely to the mountain side.

B. Her crystal ring was bright.

Her crystal ring shined like a diamond.

C. He is grouchy when he first wakes up.

He is a bear when he first wakes up in the morning.

The second line in each pair is preferred because the writer, in each case, is using a form of figurative language (repeat definition of figurative language) to bring his writing alive. (A = personification, B = simile, C = metaphor.)

Teacher: "Today we will be studying these poetic devices through their application in several different poems."

The Lesson

Input/Model:

Teacher passes out worksheet and gives a definition of simile, metaphor and personification. After each definition teacher offers a model of the device:

Simile—identifies two items that are different, but they share a quality, such as softness (i.e., Her skin was as soft as velvet). Items are often linked with the words "as" or "like."

Metaphor—again, two items that are different, but they share a quality, such as irritation (i.e. Joe is a real problem in class). Items are sometimes linked with the word "is." However, the word "is" may not be used when the comparison is obvious (i.e., The cowboy's tanned leather face looked up at the sky). Note: If students struggle with this concept, bringing in items, such as sandpaper, or crystals, and using them as examples for writing similes and metaphors may be very helpful.

Personification—when a poet attributes characteristics that are decisively human to a non-human entity (i.e., The butterfly danced around the flower). Note: The root word of personification is "person."

Check for Understanding:

Teacher offers several lines of poetry and asks student to signal (fingers held on chest) "1" if it is an example of personification, "2" if it is a simile and "3" if it is a metaphor. If the lines do not contain any one of the three devices, students are asked to put the full palm of their hand across their chests. After each example, teacher calls on a student at random and asks that student to justify/explain his or her choice:

"Gina is as happy as a lark."

(simile) LaCroix

"Clouds are the cheeks of angels."

(metaphor) LaCroix

"Love's not Time's fool, though rosey lips and cheeks

Within his bending sickle's compass come."

(personification) William Shakespeare

"Lara's hands were as soft as velvet."

(simile) LaCroix

" . . . and the dish ran away with the spoon."

(personification) Mother Goose

"The leaves danced in the wind."

(personification) LaCroix

"Flowers are summer's crown."

(metaphor) LaCroix

"The tall tree stood as a guard at the entry."

(simile) LaCroix

"Juliet is the Sun."

(metaphor) William Shakespeare

Guided Practice:

Students, working in pairs, are given "The Seven Ages of Man" by William Shakespeare and asked to identify lines that contain any one of the three types of figurative language and to underline the key words involved in the phrase. Teacher walks the room during exercise. Students should discover the metaphor in the first line (which really extends throughout the poem) and similes in lines 8, 10, and 12. Discussion follows.

Additional Practice:

"A Split Tree Still Grows" (Excellent example of personification.)

The Wrap-Up

Closure:

Students are asked to write definitions of the three key terms covered in the Glossary portion of their notebook. Students should use their own words and support each definition with an example from the lesson, from a previous poem studied in class, or one of their own.

Independent Practice:

Students are given "He Jests at Scars" by Shakespeare. Assignment: Identify examples of personification, simile, and metaphor in the poem.
or
Students use the worksheet to find additional examples of figurative language in their textbook/other class materials.

Assessment:

Identify figurative language and offer an interpretation of Shakespeare's "Like as the Waves."
or

Write an essay, discussing Shakespeare's use of figurative language, as well as other elements of style employed by the author, to further meaning in any one of the three works studied in the lesson.

or

Write an essay comparing and contrasting "The Seven Ages of Man" and "Like as Waves."

Essay Scoring Guide (Key Resource 4.3 from Lesson 1)

Reteach:

If necessary.

Notebook Requirement:

The worksheet, any assigned writings, and all poems addressed during this lesson are to be included in the student's poetry notebook.

KEY RESOURCE 4.24

Similes, Metaphors, and Personification

Name _____   Date _____

Period _____

Simile _____

_____

Example: _____

Example: _____

Example: _____

Example: _____

Metaphor _____

_____

Example: _____

Example: _____

Example: _____

Example: _____

Personification _____

_____

Example: _____

Example: _____

Example: _____

Example: _____

KEY RESOURCE 4.25

Shakespeare Poems

*The Seven Ages of Man
from* As You Like It

by William Shakespeare

All the world's a stage,

And all the men and women merely players:

They have their exits and their entrances;

And one man in his time plays many parts,

His acts being seven ages. At first the infant,

Mewling and puking in the nurse's arms.

And then the whining school-boy, with his satchel

And shining morning face, creeping like snail

Unwillingly to school. And then the lover

sighing like furnace, with a woeful ballad

Made to his mistress' eyebrow. Then a soldier,

Full of strange oaths, and bearded like the pard,

Jealous in honour, sudden and quick in quarrel,

Seeking the bubble reputation

Even in the cannon's mouth. And then the justice,

In fair round belly with good capon lin'd,

With eyes severe, and beard of formal cut,

Full of wise saws and modern instances;

And so he plays his part. The sixth age shifts

Into the lean and slipper'd pantaloon,

With spectacles on nose and pouch on side,

His youthful hose well sav'd a world too wide

For his shrunk shank; and his big manly voice,

Turning again toward childish treble, pipes

And whistles in his sound. Last scene of all,

That ends this strange eventful history,

is second childishness and mere oblivion,

Sans teeth, sans eyes, sans taste, sans everything.

—⊸⊛⊶—

He Jests at Scars
from Romeo and Juliet

by William Shakespeare

He jests at scars, that never felt a wound.

But, soft! what light through yonder window breaks?

It is the east, and Juliet is the sun!

Arise, fair sun, and kill the envious moon,

Who is already sick and pale with grief,

That thou her maid art far more fair than she:

Be not her maid, since she is envious;

Her vestal livery is but sick and green,

And none but fools do wear it; cast it off.

It is my lady; O! it is my love:

O! that she knew she were.

She speaks, yet she says nothing: what of that?

Her eye discourses; I will answer it.

I am too bold, 'tis not to me she speaks;

Two of the fairest stars in all the heaven,

Having some business, do entreat her eyes

To twinkle in their spheres till they return.

What if her eyes were there, they in her head?

The brightness of her cheek would shame those stars

As daylight doth a lamp; her eyes in heaven

Would through the airy region stream so bright

That birds would sing and think it were not night.

See! how she leans her cheek upon her hand:

O! that I were a glove upon that hand,

That I might touch that cheek.

Like as the Waves

by William Shakespeare

Like as the waves make towards the pebbled shore,

So do minutes hasten to their end;

Each changing place with that which goes before,

In sequent toil all forwards do contend,

Nativity, once in the main of light,

Crawls to maturity, wherewith being crown'd,

Crooked eclipses 'gainst his glory flight,

And Time that gave doth now his gift confound.

Time doth transfix the flourish set on you

And delves the parallels in beauty's brow,

Feeds on the rarities of nature's truth,

And nothing stands but for his scythe to mow:

And yet to times in hope my verse shall stand,

Praising thy worth, despite his cruel hand.

KEY RESOURCE 4.26

A Split Tree Still Grows

Author Unknown

Look at me

I am old

I am the beginning of life

and life survives the seasons

spring

found me alive with wealth of earth

strangers wanted my wealth for their own

my branches cut chained and transported

over oceans

as cargo in airless chambers

rerooted in foreign soils

but my roots, my roots they grabbed

and held tight to my soul

nothing could shake them

summer

lightening lashed and cracked

whipped and split my chapped bark

licked through unprotected flesh

red sap oozed down tears

but my roots, my roots they grabbed

and held tight to my soul

nothing could shake them

autumn

forced my branches to bear precious fruit

bruised and beaten and mangled

they dangled for days upon my aching limbs

until the rotting rope gave in

to my cries

but my roots, my roots they grabbed

and held tight to my soul

nothing could shake them

winter

rain poured down

dismounting from thunders' hooves in thick white sheets

to suffocate my tender buds

hurricanes blew me

from the south to the north, east to the west

but I did not break

I bent and bowed

to weather the storm

and my roots, my roots they grabbed

and held tight to my soul

nothing could shake them

LESSON 11

"Once Upon a Midnight Dreary"—Edgar Allan Poe: His Life and Works

The Setup

Purpose:

To offer students an understanding of the relationship between a poet and his works and how that relationship plays a part when interpreting poetry.

Objective:

Students compare and contrast three poems by Edgar Allan Poe.

Materials Provided:

Teacher Notes: Lecture Notes on Edgar Allan Poe
Student Worksheet: Edgar Allan Poe
Poems: "Annabel Lee," "To Helen," "A Dream Within a Dream," and excerpt from "The Raven."

Optional Materials:

Other biographical material on the poet.

Set:

Teacher says, "His mother died when he was three and his father deserted him. He was raised by an adoptive family and plagued by psychological, physical, and spiritual demons throughout his life. Despite these adversities, he came to be one of America's great short writers and poets. His name was Edgar Allan Poe."

The Lesson

Input:

Students are given worksheet (Edgar Allan Poe) and asked to record notes as teacher goes into more details on the author's life. These details should include, but are not limited to, the information contained in the teacher lecture notes.

Many of Poe's poems were centered around the poet's obsession with romantic love. The women in his poems, Annabel Lee, Helen, and Lenore, are all women that he loved "with a love that was more than love," what we would term today an "obsession." Another characteristic that the three women share is that each one dies (as did his wife, Virginia), and there is some communication, or an attempt to communicate, between the heroines and the poet after death.

Teacher says, "Today we will take a close look at three Poe poems involving this story line."

Students are given copies of the poems "Annabel Lee," "To Helen," and excerpts from "The Raven."

Model:

Teacher reads the first stanza of "To Helen." The first stanza is clearly a remark on Helen's beauty, a beauty that is classic ("Nicean barks of yore"— reference to the Ancient Greeks) and immortal (as the tides—"gently, o'er a perfumed sea"). In Stanza 2, the poet returns to Helen ("to the glory that was Greece and the grandeur that was Rome"). In the third stanza they are reunited, but she is clearly dead ("how statue-like"—stiffness of death).

Guided Practice/Check for Understanding:

Students work in pairs on "The Raven." They are asked to analyze/interpret the stanzas as they apply to this pervasive author theme. (Speaker in a room reading and visited by his love, the lost Lenore.) Class discusses findings.

Guided Practice/Check for Understanding:

Students work independently on "Annabel Lee." They are asked to use their analysis skills and knowledge of the author to interpret the stanzas. Class discusses findings.

The Wrap-Up

Closure:

Students write a paragraph comparing and contrasting the three Poe poems.

Independent Practice and Assessment:

Students analyze the poem "A Dream Within a Dream."
or
Students are asked to memorize portions of the poems. Suggestions: (1) Three stanzas of "Annabel Lee"—the first, the last, and one other of their choosing, (2) all of the stanzas in "to Helen," or (3) the first and last excerpted stanzas from "The Raven."

Reteach:

If necessary.

Notebook Requirement:

All worksheets and poems are to be added to the poetry notebook.

Additional Resources:

There are several videos that feature representations of Poe and his works and there are compact discs that contain songs written as companion pieces to his poems. They are available in some libraries or can be ordered from book and video stores.

Added Note:

"Lecture Notes on Edgar Allan Poe" is intended as a resource for the teacher, but it may be used as a student handout as well.

KEY RESOURCE 4.27

Lecture Notes on Edgar Allan Poe

Lived 1809–1849.

One of the greatest critics, short story writers, and poets to write in the nineteenth century.

Mother died when he was three, father deserted him, and he was raised by adopted family (the Allans). He took Allan as his middle name.

Most famous poem: "The Raven"

A little known fact: He was also the father of the modern mystery ("Who done it?") stories.

Other short stories included tales of terror.

Attended the University of Virginia for some time, but then became involved in gambling and left.

Spent some time in West Point but was forced to resign because he broke regulations.

Went to work as a magazine editor and critic.

Married his cousin, Virginia Clemm, when she was fourteen.

1847—Virginia died and Poe began to drink heavily.

1849—Poe became engaged to his childhood sweetheart.

Before they married, Poe died. He was found dead, lying in the streets of Baltimore.

The cause of his death continues to be a mystery.

KEY RESOURCE 4.28

Name _____   Date _____

Period _____

Edgar Allan Poe

Once upon a midnight dreary, while I pondered, weak and weary,

Over many a quaint and curious volume of forgotten lore,

While I nodded, nearly napping, suddenly there came a tapping,

As of some one gently rapping, rapping at my chamber door.

Excerpt from "the Raven"

Notes:

_____

_____

_____

_____

_____

_____

_____

_____

_____

_____

_____

_____

_____

_____

KEY RESOURCE 4.29

Annabel Lee

by Edgar Allan Poe

It was many and many a year ago,

In a kingdom by the sea,

That a maiden there lived whom you may know

By the name of Annabel Lee;—

And this maiden she lived with no other thought

Than to love and be loved by me.

She was a child and I was a child,

In this kingdom by the sea,

But we loved with a love that was more than love—

I and my Annabel Lee—

With a love that the winged seraphs of heaven

Coveted her and me.

And this was the reason that, long ago,

In this kingdom by the sea,

A wind blew out of a cloud by night

Chilling my Annabel Lee;

So that her high-born kinsman came

And bore her away from me,

To shut her up in a sepulcher

In this kingdom by the sea.

The angels, not half so happy in Heaven,

Went envying her and me;—

Yes! that was the reason (as all men know,

In this kingdom by the sea)

That the wind came out of a cloud, chilling

And killing my Annabel Lee.

But our love it was stronger by far than the love

Of those who were older than we—

Of many far wiser than me—

And neither the angels in Heaven above,

Nor the demons down under the sea,

Can ever dissever my soul from the soul

Of the beautiful Annabel Lee;—

For the moon never beams without bringing me dreams

Of the beautiful Annabel Lee;

And the stars never rise but I see the bright eyes

Of the beautiful Annabel Lee;

And so, all the night-tide, I lie down by the side

Of my darling, my darling, my life and my bride,

In her sepulcher there by the sea—

In her tomb by the side of the sea.

KEY RESOURCE 4.30

To Helen

by Edgar Allan Poe

Helen, thy beauty is to me

Like those Nicean barks of yore,

That gently, o'er a perfumed sea,

The weary, wayworn wanderer bore

To his own native shore.

On desperate seas long wont to roam,

Thy hyacinth hair, thy classic face,

Thy Naiad airs have brought home

To the glory that was Greece

And the grandeur that was Rome.

Lo! in yon brilliant window-niche

How statue-like I see thee stand,

The agate lamp within thy hand!

Ah, Psyche, from the regions which

Are Holy Land!

KEY RESOURCE 4.31

A Dream Within a Dream

by Edgar Allan Poe

Take this kiss upon the brow!

And, in parting from you now,

Thus much let me avow—

You are not wrong, who deem

That my days have been a dream;

Yet if hope has flown away

In a night, or in a day,

In a vision, or in none,

Is it therefore the less gone?

All that we see or seem

Is but a dream within a dream.

I stand amid the roar

Of a surf-tormented shore,

And I hold within my hand

Grains of the golden sand—

How few! yet how they creep

Through my fingers to the deep,

While I weep—while I weep!

O God! can I not grasp

Them with a tighter clasp?

O God! can I not save

One from the pitiless wave?

Is all that we see or seem

But a dream within a dream?

KEY RESOURCE 4.32

Excerpt From "The Raven"

by Edgar Allan Poe

Stanza 1

Once upon a midnight dreary, while I pondered, weak and weary,

Over many a quaint and curious volume of forgotten lore,

While I nodded, nearly napping, suddenly there came a tapping,

As of some one gently rapping, rapping at my chamber door.

"This some visitor," I muttered, "tapping at my chamber door—

Only this, and nothing more."

Stanza 2

Ah distinctly I remember it was in the bleak December,

And each separate dying ember wrought its ghost upon the floor.

Eagerly I wished the morrow;— vainly I had sought to borrow

From my books surcease of sorrow—sorrow for the lost Lenore—

For the rare and radiant maiden whom the angels name Lenore—

Nameless here for evermore.

Stanza 5

Deep into that darkness peering, long I stood there wondering, fearing,

Doubting, dreaming dreams no mortals ever dared to dream before;

But the silence was unbroken, and the stillness gave no token,

And the only word there spoken was the whispered word, "Lenore!"

This whispered, and an echo murmured back the word, "Lenore!"—

Merely this, and nothing more.

LESSON 12

Life's Lessons in Verse

Though nothing can bring back the hour
Of splendour in the grass, of glory in the flower

The Setup

Purpose:

To offer students an understanding and appreciation for poetry that teaches life's lessons.

Objective:

Students will study several poems to determine the lessons offered.

Materials Provided:

Worksheet: Teaching Poems
Poems: "The Village Blacksmith" by Henry Wadsworth Longfellow; "To thine own self be true," an excerpt from *Hamlet* by William Shakespeare; "If Tomorrow Never Comes" (author unknown); "O Great Spirit" (author unknown); excerpt from "Ode: Intimations of Immortality" by William Wordsworth; "To be, or not to be," an excerpt from *Hamlet* by William Shakespeare
Essay Scoring Guide (Key Resource 4.3 from Lesson 1)

Optional Materials:

Poems: "The Trouble Was Meals" by Elizabeth Bennett; "Tribal Cemetery" by Janet Campbell Hale; "Into the Sun" by Hannah Kahn; "Be Nobody's Darling" by Alice Walker

Set:

When we studied the works of Edgar Allan Poe, we read a poem titled "Annabel Lee." This poem told a story and is a genre of verse known as narrative poetry. Today we will be looking at another genre of verse, in which the poet attempts to teach one of life's lessons. We will refer to it as teaching poetry.

The Lesson

Input/Model:

Students are given "Teaching Poems" worksheet to which they add the definition of the genre, poetry that teaches a life lesson. Teacher discusses model of genre, excerpt from "Ode . . ." by William Wordsworth.

The author is teaching the reader to celebrate nature ("sing a joyous song"), to commune with nature ("ye that pipe and ye that play"), and to be one with nature ("Ye that through your hearts to-day/Feel the gladness of the May").

The poet draws a comparison in which nature takes on an even greater significance, becoming "the radiance" (the idealism of youth) "which was once so bright" (radiance grows dimmer, idealism of the youth becomes the practical realities of the old) and is now "for ever taken from . . . sight,"
concluding with . . .

"Though nothing can bring back the hour

Of splendour in the grass, of glory in the flower"

Check for Understanding and Guided Practice:

Students are arranged into cooperative groups of four. Each group member is given a copy of one of the following poems: "The Village Blacksmith," "To thine own self be true," "If Tomorrow Never Comes," and "O Great Spirit," as well as a "Teaching Poems" worksheet.

All students read their individual poems silently (each member of the group has a different poem), and then aloud to their group, integrating the elements of a good dramatic reading. After each poem is read, the group members discuss their understanding of the lesson the poet is teaching and record that conclusion on their worksheets.

After all students have shared with their group, students take their poems and move into other groups composed of students who are sharing the same poem. Students share the findings of their group regarding the lesson offered by the poet. They return to their original groups and report back their findings. Some may reconsider their original assumptions about the poem and edit at this time.

Teacher walks room, checking for understanding and offering support where needed.

Students are now asked to prepare to read and discuss the poems with the whole class. Although all students have prepared, teacher calls on only one person to present each of the four poems, offering a dramatic reading and an analysis of the lesson. Class discussion follows each presentation.

Teacher Notes:

Answers may vary from student to student and group to group. The purpose of the assignment is to prompt discussion of the poems. In general, if an assumption can be supported by text, it is correct.

The Wrap-Up

Closure:

Students record definition and chosen example of teaching poetry.
and/or
Students are asked to write a paragraph naming and defending one of the four poems in the series as the "best" poem.

Independent Practice:

Students are given a copy of the excerpt from *Hamlet*, "To be, or not to be," and asked to write a paragraph defending the verse as a teaching poem.
and/or
Students write an essay discussing teaching poetry as a verse genre, including excerpts from three poems, which are outside (not used in this lesson) examples.

Assessment:

Thursday Quiz
Essay Scoring Guide (Key Resource 4.3 from Lesson 1)

Reteach:

If necessary.

Notebook Requirement:

Students should be given clean copies of all four of the poems addressed in the group work and add these, along with their completed worksheet, to the notebook.

KEY RESOURCE 4.33

Teaching Poems

Name _____

Date _____

Definition: _____

Excerpt from "Ode: Intimations of Immortality" by William Wordsworth

Then sing, ye Birds, sing, sing a joyous song!

And let the young Lambs bound

As to the tabor's sound!

We in thought will join your throng,

Ye that pipe and ye that play,

Ye that through your hearts to-day

Feel the gladness of the May!

What though the radiance which was once so bright

Be now forever taken from my sight,

Though nothing can bring back the hour

Of splendour in the grass, of glory in the flower;

Lesson: _____

_____

_____

Evidence: _____

_____

_____

_____

"The Village Blacksmith"
by Henry Wadsworth Longfellow

Lesson: _____

_____

_____

Evidence: _____

_____

_____

_____

"To thine own self be true"
(from *Hamlet*) by William Shakespeare

Lesson: _____

_____

_____

Evidence: _____

_____

_____

_____

"If Tomorrow Never Comes," Author Unknown

Lesson: _____

_____

_____

Evidence: _____

_____

_____

_____

"O Great Spirit," Author Unknown

Lesson: _____

_____

_____

Evidence: _____

_____

_____

_____

"O Great Spirit," Author Unknown

KEY RESOURCE 4.34

The Village Blacksmith

by Henry Wadsworth Longfellow

Under a spreading chestnut tree
The village smithy stands;
The smith, a mighty man is he,
With large and sinewy hands;
And the muscles on his brawny arms
Are as strong as iron bands.

His hair is crisp, and black and long,
His face is like the tan;
His brow is wet with honest sweat,
He earns whate'er he can,
And looks the whole world in the face,
For he owes not any man.

Week in, week out, from morn till night,
You can hear his bellows blow;
You can hear him swing his heavy sledge,
With a measured beat and slow,
Like a sexton ringing the village bell,
When the evening sun is low.

And children coming home from school
Look in at the open door;
They love to see the flaming forge,
And hear the bellows roar,
And catch the burning sparks that fly
Like chaff from a threshing floor.

He goes on Sunday to the church,

And sits among his boys;

He hears the parson pray and preach,

He hears his daughter's voice,

Singing in the village choir,

And it makes his heart rejoice.

It sounds to him like her mother's voice,

Singing in Paradise;

He needs must think of her once more,

How in the grave she lies;

And with his hard rough hand he wipes

A tear out of his eyes.

Toiling-rejoicing-sorrowing,

Onward through life he goes;

Each morning sees some task begin,

Each evening sees it close;

Something attempted, something done,

Has earned a night's repose.

Thanks, thanks to thee, my worthy friend,

For the lesson thou hast taught!

Thus at the flaming forge of life

Our fortunes must be wrought;

Thus on its sounding anvil shaped

Each burning deed and thought.

KEY RESOURCE 4.35

To thine own self be true

from *Hamlet* by William Shakespeare

There, my blessings with thee!

And these few precepts in thy memory

Look thou character. Give thy thoughts no tongue,

Nor any unproportioned thought his act.

Be thou familiar, but by no means vulgar;

The friends thou hast, and their adoption tried,

Grapple them to thy soul with hoops of steel;

But do not dull thy palm with entertainment

Of each new-hatched, unfledged comrade. Beware

Of entrance to a quarrel, but, being in,

Bear't that the opposed may beware of thee.

Give every man thine ear, but few thy voice;

Take each man's censure, but reserve thy judgement.

Costly thy habit as thy purse can buy,

But not expressed in fancy; rich, not gaudy;

For the apparel oft proclaims the man,

And they in France of the best rank and station

Are most select and generous, chief in that.

Neither a borrower, nor a lender be;

For loan oft loses both itself and friend,

And borrowing dulls the edge of husbandry.

This above all: to thine own self be true,

And it must follow, as the night the day,

Thou canst not then be false to any man.

KEY RESOURCE 4.36

If Tomorrow Never Comes

Author Unknown

If I knew it would be the last time
that I'd see you fall asleep,
I would tuck you in more tightly
and pray the Lord, your soul to keep.

If I knew it would be the last time
that I see you walk out the door,
I would give you a hug and kiss
and call you back for one more.

If I knew it would be the last time
I'd hear your voice lifted in praise,
I would video tape each action and word,
so I could play them back day after day.

If I knew it would be the last time,
I could spare an extra minute or two
to stop and say "I love you,"
instead of assuming you would know I do.

If I knew it would be the last time
I would be there to share your day,
well I'm sure you'll have so many more,
so I can let just this one slip away.

For surely there's always tomorrow
to make up for an oversight,
and we always get a second chance
to make everything right.

There will always be another day
to say our "I love you's,"
And certainly there's another chance
to say our "Anything I can do's?"

But just in case I might be wrong,
and today is all I get,
I'd like to say how much I love you
and I hope we never forget.

Tomorrow is not promised to anyone,
young or old alike,
And today may be the last chance
you get to hold your loved one tight.

So if you're waiting for tomorrow,
why not do it today?
For if tomorrow never comes,
you'll surely regret the day.

That you didn't take that extra time
for a smile, a hug, or a kiss
and you were too busy to grant someone,
what turned out to be their one last wish.

So hold your loved ones close today,
whisper in their ear,
Tell them how much you love them
and that you'll always hold them dear.

Take time to say "I'm sorry," "please forgive me,"
"thank you" or "it's okay."
And if tomorrow never comes,
you'll have no regrets about today.

KEY RESOURCE 4.37

O Great Spirit

(from Native American poetry)

Author Unknown

O Great Spirit
Whose voice I hear in the winds,
And whose breath gives life to all the world,
Hear me!
I am small and weak, I need your strength and wisdom.

Let me walk in beauty,
Make my eyes
Ever behold the red and purple sunset.
Make my hands respect the things you have made
And my ears sharp to hear Your voice.

Make me wise
So that I may understand the things
You have taught my people.
Let me learn the lessons
You have hidden in every leaf and rock.

I seek strength,
Not to be greater than my brother,
But to fight my greatest enemy
—my selfishness.

Make me always ready to come to You
With clean hands and straight eyes.
So when life fades, as the fading sunset,
My spirit may come to You without shame.

Bless the wisdom of the Holy One above us;
Bless the truth of the Holy One beneath us;
Bless the love of the Holy One within us.

KEY RESOURCE 4.38

To be, or not to be

Excerpt from *Hamlet* by William Shakespeare

To be, or not to be: that is the question:

Whether tis nobler in the mind to suffer

The slings and arrows of outrageous fortune,

Or to take arms against a sea of troubles,

And by opposing end them? To die; to sleep;

No more; and, by a sleep to say we end

The heart-ache and the thousand natural; shocks

That flesh is heir to, 'tis a consummation

Devoutly to be wished. To die, to sleep;

To sleep: perchance to dream: aye, there's the rub;

For in that sleep of death what dreams may come

When we have shuffled off this mortal coil,

Must give us pause, There's the respect

That makes calamity of so long life;

For who would bear the whips and scorns of time,

The oppressor's wrong, the proud man's contumely,

The pangs of disprized love, the law's delay,

The insolence of office, and the spurns

That patient merit of the unworthy takes,

When he himself might his quietus make

With a bare bobkin? who would fardels bear,

To grunt and sweat under a weary life,

But that the dread of something after death,

The undiscovered country from whose bourn

No traveller returns, puzzles the will,

And makes us rather bear those ills we have

Than fly to others that we know not of?

Thus conscience does make cowards of us all;

And thus the native hue of resolution

Is sicklied o'er with the pale cast of thought,

And enterprises of great pith and moment

With this regard their currents turn awry,

And lose the name of action.

LESSON 13

A Poetry Potpourri

It has been difficult for me to decide which strategies and materials to use as I wrote the poetry unit. I chose each lesson very carefully and each poem quite deliberately. And, for every lesson and poem I included, there were another three that I sadly left behind.

Henry David Thoreau wrote, "he who travels with another must wait till the other is ready." I have chosen to take this poet's advice and to end our journey here, with the last poetry lesson yet to be written. I leave you then, with a few ideas, my parting gifts to you . . .

- ☞ Build a lesson around "Dreams." Use "Dreams" by Langston Hughes and "Always Hold on to Your Dreams" by Nancye Sims as starters.

- ☞ Build a lesson around "Cat" poems. Students love Gary Soto's "Ode to Mi Gato" and Rod McKuen's "A Cat Named Sloopy."

- ☞ Poems written by other teens are often well received. Consider "Comes the Dawn," "Please Listen," and "Paint Brush" by B. B. Youngs.

- ☞ Teach a lesson on image poems. Two great examples are "Oranges" by Gary Soto and "Waitin on Summer" by Ruth Forman.

- ☞ Consider recording the lyrics of songs and presenting them in the form of a poem. This lesson emphasizes the connection between poetry and music. I often begin reading the poetic lyrics to "Eleanor Rigby" by John Lennon and Paul McCartney and then playing the song by the Beatles.

- ☞ "If I Were in Charge of the World" by Judith Viorst is a great poem that students easily identify with and are able to rewrite (as a formula poem) using their own ideas.

- ☞ Spend time considering Walt Whitman's "O Captain! My Captain" (on the death of President Lincoln). It is an excellent example of a poem that reflects the author's feelings, as well as the events of the time.

- ☞ Teach a lesson emphasizing an author's use of capitalization, rhyme scheme, line breaks, and repetition. Consider how these elements contribute to the overall effect/meaning of the poem.

- ☞ A poem that I consider to be the "All American Poem" is Theyer's "Casey at the Bat." If at all possible, find a way to include it in your lessons.

- ☞ Incorporate writing by having students study two related poems extensively and then writing a compare-and-contrast essay on the poems.

- ☞ Use "Sir Gawain and the Green Knight" (medieval verse; one of King Arthur's knights) to teach narrative poetry, alliterative verse, and symbolism.

- Design a lesson around Native American poetry.

- Design lessons incorporating the works of Langston Hughes or Maya Angelou (or both). Poems by these authors are well received by young adults.

Project

- As a final in-class or take-home exam, have students complete a Scavenger Hunt, using the poems in their poetry books (or not). This exposes them to more examples of the elements you have taught. For instance: Find five good examples of personification, fifteen good examples of metaphors, and so on.

The Final Touches **5**

Make the road, and others will make the journey . . .

Victor Hugo

SUGGESTIONS FOR A SUCCESSFUL POETRY RECITAL

Reading and writing about works of fiction is an ongoing process in almost every language arts classroom. Traditionally, time may be taken to teach a unit on journalism, a unit on creative writing, or a unit on poetry. These separate units of study, unlike the teaching of fiction (the meat and potatoes of the English classroom), are generally built around a culminating activity, an event that marks the end of study and celebrates student success.

Usually a unit of study in poetry ends with a recital. This event is an excellent way to celebrate our journey's end.

It is key that the poetry recital not be considered another Poetry Circle. This is the students' culminating activity, an opportunity for them to present to their classmates, to their parents, and even to members of the community, what they have learned. There is no one way to conduct a recital; however, every successful classroom recital does contain essential components. They are as follows:

- The recital is to be viewed as a serious undertaking. Do not allow any student to trivialize the event.

- Each class should have their own recital. If you are teaching five classes of language arts/English, the general rule of thumb should be that you plan for five recitals. Allow each one of your classes the opportunity to perform separately. This offers the students a larger pool of poems from which to choose. For instance, a poem can be read only once during a recital. A popular poem such as "Comes the Dawn" could be read by different students at different recitals. Another consideration is that you want to put a reasonable time limit on the recital. It is possible to hear thirty poems within an hour's time, but certainly not sixty. Finally, by offering each class its own presentation, you are honoring the students who have worked so hard to prepare for the event.

- The recital should be held in a location other than the classroom. By moving the recital to another location, you emphasize the importance of the event. You are saying in a very real way, "I'm proud of you and the work you have done during the course of this unit." I have successfully held recitals in school auditoriums or in corners of shaded areas of the campus with chairs set up for the audience. Another excellent option would be to contact your local bookstore and inquire about holding the recital in their store.

- The teacher must approve the poems the students chose for the recital (like the weekly Poetry Circle poems). They are not, however, restricted from reading the poems they have studied in class. They are free to choose poems they have delivered in the Poetry Circle, poems that they have studied in class, poems that interest them and speak to their sensibilities, and even poems that they have authored. The only requirement is that they be approved beforehand.

- After the students have selected the poems and the teacher approved them, the students should practice, practice, practice. This practice can take place at school before different groups of students, at home before the mirror, or before friends and family.

- There should be at least one rehearsal at the site of the recital.

- Mandate that all students participate in the recital and that they each perform separately. There have been those times when I have allowed a reading from "two voices" or "three voices." These paired or group readings were approved on a case-by-case basis. For instance, a student who is bilingual may want to read a poem in his or her primary language and work with another reader who follows him or her, presenting the poem in English. I have occasionally allowed three students to present. In one case, the poem was long (Angelou's "On the Pulse of Morning"), and three students presented the poem, each one symbolically representing the river, the rock, or the tree. At times they each read separately and at other times they read together. I have also allowed groups of three to present a longer narrative poem. It should be noted that choral readings are the exception, not the norm. Every effort should be made to encourage individual readings.

- Invitations to other classes, administrators, parents, and the community should be sent out at least one week prior to the recital. (A student should be in charge of designing the invitation.)

- A program should be made and handed out to the audience as they enter. (Students should be stationed at the entry, welcoming guests and handing them a program as they enter.)

- The "stage" should contain a lectern and a vase with one red rose. Depending on the location of the recital, you may or may not want to employ a microphone. Other than these three items, no other props should be allowed. The purpose of the recital is to enjoy the reader's vocal presentation, to be stirred by the voice that brings meaning to the poem.

- If your presentation is to be held in an auditorium, the lights should be dimmed, and there should be one spotlight directed toward the reader.

- You can plan for a student to assume the role of master of ceremonies, announcing each presentation. Another option would be to have students (presenters) introduce the next reading after they have presented.

- Recognize participants by presenting each with a "Poetic License." See sample at the end of the chapter.

- Applause should be held until the end when all readers return to the stage and take a bow. Return to the stage with them; you deserve applause as well.

KEY RESOURCE 5.1

Poetic License

Fill in this area with a poem or excerpt of the piece presented by the student at the recital.

Poetic license is awarded to _____

in accordance with the provisions of lyric expression

on this _____ day of _____ in the year of _____ .

This license entitles the bearer to read, analyze, compose, and present poetry in all diverse forms.

This license is issued with distinction and in celebration of the holder's success while undertaking the study of the art of poetry.

Signed by my hand _____
(teacher's signature)

School _____

City _____

State _____

(Frame with a creative border)

Closing
Letter to Reader

Dear Reader:

As I write these last lines to you, I am reminded that I am one of those who can never quite envision a journey's end—until I have almost arrived. Perhaps because I have taught these lessons and recited these words for so long, I now find myself surprised to realize this journey's end.

My best wishes go with you as you take these lessons I have offered and make them your own. Know that other muses wait for you as your journey continues, ready to guide you along the way.

I will be with you in spirit, my fellow traveler.

Lorraine LaCroix

Index

**CORWIN
PRESS**

The Corwin Press logo—a raven striding across an open book—represents the union of courage and learning. Corwin Press is committed to improving education for all learners by publishing books and other professional development resources for those serving the field of K–12 education. By providing practical, hands-on materials, Corwin Press continues to carry out the promise of its motto: **"Helping Educators Do Their Work Better."**